MY SOUL SHOWED UP

PAT HENNEBERRY

Helping talented writers
publish exceptional books.

This book is a memoir. It reflects the author's present recollections of experiences over time. Some names and characteristics have been changed, some events have been compressed, and some dialogue has been recreated. The author in no way represents any company, corporation, or brand mentioned herein.

Contents

Author's Note   vii

Part One
When You Fall Mid-Flight
1. The Fall   3
2. An Encounter With Hope   15
3. The Big Kahuna   31
4. Face the Storm Like an Eagle   45
5. The Greatest Hero   57
6. Even Titanium Breaks   66
7. Another Walk at Dawn   84

Part Two
The Comeback
8. Basement Walking   97
9. New Dreams   105
10. The Loneliness Precipice   115
11. Show Up   135
12. Leave Your Ego at The Door   146
13. Expand Your Think Threshold   157
14. Why Is it So Hard to Ask for Help?   169
15. Be a Badass   186

Part Three
My Soul Showed Up
16. Sailing Through It   197
17. Sitting in this Season   209
18. A New Kind of Gym   213
19. Burning the Beads   220
20. Search for Hope   225

21. Practice Compassion & Empathy   235
22. Own Your Story   246
23. Silver Linings   255
24. My Miracles   261
25. The Enigma of the End   275

  Epilogue: Dear Rebel   283
  Acknowledgments   285
  About the Author   289
  Pat's Power Playlist   291

To my mother, Marion Henneberry,
who has held up the light through every season of my life.

Author's Note

Many personal stories are written from a bird's eye point of view. There is a beginning, middle, and end that time has allowed the writer to be partially removed from. Perhaps they are writing a story about something that happened five, ten, or even twenty-five years earlier. They've been given time to reflect, analyze, and gain insight into their experiences.

Then there's the other way, the way I wrote this book, right in the midst of it all, realizing I needed to be documenting this if, for no other reason, but to help grasp some answers as to the constant hurdles being thrown my way.

This book is the culmination of the notes I journaled and the voice memos I recorded during my journey. Along the way, I would realize a truth that would inspire me to keep moving forward, to keep showing up. That nugget of hope would be jotted down. People would ask me about my story, and I began sharing with them these nuggets I was learning. Often, I would see tears well up in their eyes or sense a spark lighting up their hearts, and that's when I knew what I was

writing was not meant for me alone. These truths are sprin-
kled throughout the book, and often highlighted at the end of
chapters. May you connect with them while you go about
your day overcoming so many things that are often out of
your control, and realizing you are so much stronger than
you know.

—Pat

"We must not be content only to see things as they are. We must have the vision, faith, and hope to see what things can and must become."

—Sister Generose Gervais, administrator of St. Mary's Hospital 1971-1986

Part One

When You Fall Mid-Flight

Chapter 1

The Fall

I get my sense of humor from my mom and my competitive edge from my dad. This rings true in all of my memories. My mom loved to tease my dad, and because of that so much of their marriage was playing jokes on one another. My two sisters and I were not protected from this, so the Henneberry home became a dwelling of practical jokesters.

I grew up in a supportive neighborhood in Urbandale, Iowa where we knew every person on our block. We celebrated each family's victories, supported one another during the hard moments, and made a whole bunch of memories along the way. Every summer, our neighborhood had a produce competition (welcome to Iowa) to see who could grow the biggest tomato on the vine and who could grow the largest cucumber. Each family's largest offerings would be measured and a winner declared on the 4th of July.

One year, my dad was determined to grow the biggest cucumber. With his full intention set on this, he read up on and grilled his uncles who had grown up on family farms for tips on how to accomplish such a noble feat. Us kids and my mom didn't hear the end of it. He loved to share what he was learning and fully believed if he just worked hard enough, he would meet his goal.

My mom found his boasting fuel for her talents and decided to mess with him. Two weeks before the competition, while buying her weekly groceries from Hy-Vee, she bought a cucumber much larger than any that were currently growing in my dad's intention-setting garden. That night she went down to his plot and placed the store-bought cucumber amongst the others, wrapping a vine around it to make it look like it was growing with the others, and making sure to take off the Hy-Vee sticker that was on it.

The next morning, my dad barged into the kitchen whooping and hollering about this one giant cucumber which had a growth spurt overnight. His enthusiasm was contagious as he was sure none of our neighbors could compete with this beauty.

The next night my mom did it again with a slightly bigger cucumber. And the following night she did the same thing. She kept doing this every single night until the competition, building up my dad's confidence while doing her best to maintain a poker face that wouldn't spoil the moment she was waiting for. On the final night, she placed in the garden bed the largest store cucumber she'd ever seen, but this time left the Hy-Vee sticker on the bottom of it. She could barely sleep that night in giddy anticipation of the next day.

My mom, bless her, couldn't help but tell my sisters and I, and *all of our neighbors* of her prank. Thus, on the day of judgment, the only one not in on the joke was my dad. As a neighborhood, we went around to each house, watching each contestant pick their best tomato and cucumber, and hand them over for weight and measurement. As we jaunted over to my house, there was a great hush amongst all of our neighbors as we all tried to hold in giggles. We watched as my dad, proud as ever, bent down to pick up his prized cucumber only to be met with the betrayal of a Hy-Vee sticker affixed to it. The look on his face when he saw that sticker was priceless—shock then fury, a shade of embarrassment paired with amusement, and concluding with awe at what he knew was my mom's ability to pull one over on him after all these years. Our whole neighborhood erupted in a roar of laughter, tears streaming down our faces. I'll never forget it.

These are the moments that built the woman I am, and in my new season of life are ones I hold close to me. I've learned the most sacred minutes of our lives are often the ones we don't snap a picture of. They are the seconds that our memory has to rev up into full gear, reminding us who we are and what we were created for.

There are other moments we might, at first glance, want to forget. Those standout moments in life where you feel your life's trajectory shift, whether you want it to or not. It's when your plans for the future are suddenly derailed by something outside of your power. It's the phone call in the middle of the night that someone you loved has suddenly passed. Or the day you lose your job and the identity your work gave you. Or the moment the doctor gives you a dire prognosis. No one is immune to life's losses. We can't control the upheavals that God, the Universe, or our DNA will throw our way, but we can control how we react to these seismic events.

This brings me to the morning of April 9th, 2017. If you had asked me about where I was in the pursuit of my dreams that morning, I would've told you I was on fire. Maybe not those exact words, but it would've been implied.

I was in the top tier of the diamond selling industry, and because of that my job was flying me all across the world to use my love of storytelling to speak to thousands of people in the hopes that they would be inspired to pursue their own calling.

I was thriving on the athleticism of my body, accomplishing large summit hikes and triathlons, and playing tennis regularly with an incredible group of people. I lived in a beautiful home in a community called Lakeway, just outside of the amazing city of Austin, Texas. I had recently accomplished my dream of owning a lot on Lake Travis where I was building the perfect dock to take open swims off of and to park my sailboat at.

I had clear purpose in my life. On top of my work, I was a lifelong swimmer, and had taken my passion for the sport and donated my time as the local Special Olympics swim team coach. I coached with a motto that this wasn't just about participation but was about giving these athletes a shot to compete, to be truly great, all while having fun.

I had an amazing community of friends and an Irish Catholic family I loved deeply. I was a dependable friend, and my social calendar was filled with days on the dock, open water swims, and tennis with amazing women.

I was independent and proud of that. Though I would've loved a spouse, I was proud of all I had accomplished on my own. And I was open to bringing someone into my life if the right person arrived.

I was full of hope, and the hope came easy, naturally, just as it should.

On the afternoon of April 9th, 2017, I was cruising through my neighborhood in my latest purchase—a brand new (to me), souped-up golf cart. It had yellow and black racing stripes, designer yellow wheel hubs, and the message, *Good Vibes Only*, painted on the front. I was just rolling around on my street, trying to look as cool as I felt in my cute and sporty golf cart.

One of my Special Olympic swimmers, Jenee, lived around the corner. She was a twenty-two-year-old with Down syndrome and an infectious laugh and beautiful smile.

"Do you want to ride with me?"

"Yes, please!" Jenee was thrilled with my invitation.

And with that, we jetted around the neighborhood, laughing so hard when I drove over a bumpy part of the road and we almost fell out.

That golf cart ride was one of those perfect moments where you stop and think to yourself, "I can't believe this is my life," and gratitude oozes from your pores. This was *the* good life. This was why I worked so hard—so that I could share my successes with others, and we could laugh about it time and time again.

Around 6pm, I dropped Jenee back off at her house, and headed to my home just down the street. Home was always my safe place, and as I parked my golf cart in the perfectly laid out spot I had plotted for in my garage, I couldn't get my smile to leave my face. It was a permanent fixture.

As I entered my house, I was ready for a wonderful night of me-time. I was planning on heating up one of my favorite frozen dinners and enjoying a lovely glass of wine while I unwound from the day. I replayed the memories of the golf cart ride with Jenee, and I giggled out loud while walking down my hallway to a small foyer in the middle of my house. Everything was just right until...*bam!* A loud thud sounded as a pain so unexpected and horrific hit my body that my knees slammed down on the wood floor of the foyer. With no warning, my left leg felt like a bomb had just exploded in my muscles. I lay on the ground, feral noises coming out of my mouth as I tried to grasp what happened.

What could have happened to my body from the garage to the foyer? Did I tear a muscle or something?

Though I wanted to search for an answer, the pain was all consuming. My deductive reasoning took a seat as I tried to slow my breathing, desperately praying that this feeling would go away. But it didn't. It stayed with me like a leech with no intention to leave the coziness it must've found my body to be.

As I was writhing in pain on my foyer floor, I eventually realized one thing: I needed help, and I needed it fast. Luckily, my phone was still by my side. I called two of my closest friends, Marty and Veronica (our families had known each other for forty years). Marty came immediately, and when I saw his car pull up, my heart leapt and my stomach sunk. I was so grateful for help, but I had no idea how I was going to get to the car.

Mind over matter, I crawled toward the door at a snail's pace. Thankfully I was only a few feet away, but with each inch I conquered, my brain pounded with the reality that I didn't know pain could be so intense. The throbbing in my left leg was like being hit over and over again by a bolt of lightning. Nothing had prepared me for agony like this.

Miraculously, I made it outside desperate to see Marty, one of the gentlest, smartest men I knew who had a voice of reason that would make everything right. Despite the searing pain, I didn't think this was going to be a big deal. The plan in my head was: First, stop the pain. Second, find the fix. Third, get back to my life. Marty would help me figure this out. But as I watched my friend's face take me in, and I saw Marty's default expression of calm and reason turn to one of shock, I knew this was serious.

I was completely hunched over as I couldn't straighten my back, but Marty helped me make it into his car, a feat so painful I thought I was going to black out, and drove me toward the nearest emergency room. I felt like I was in a daze. *How is this happening? This isn't my life.*

At the hospital, Marty found me a wheelchair because I truly couldn't walk on my own. I was slumped over sitting in it when I finally got admitted. The ER staff pumped me up with morphine and every pain medicine they could, but I kept asking for more. I never imagined my motto of *more* relating to morphine, but nothing was making a dent in this debilitating pain.

At nine p.m., my best friend, Joanna, showed up and talked Marty into going home.

"I'll stay, and go home with Pat," she said.

After being there for eight hours, the ER had no answers or solutions for my situation, so they decided to send me home. I was hysterical, crying and outraged at being discharged. It was a strange position as I had always been the cool, calm, collected one. I was always a dependable friend helping others. I was none of those at that moment.

"I'm in more pain than when I came in. It's getting worse, not better. Please, help me!" I cried to the attending doctor.

"Ma'am, there's nothing more for us to do. You need to see an orthopedic surgeon." His words drained any immediate hope for release from pain's grip, and I received the message: You're somebody else's problem.

Joanna took me home and spent the night with me, attending to my every need. The next day she drove me to get an injection in my back to see if it could lessen my discomfort. While at the doctor's office, I was so uncomfortable that I maneuvered out of the wheelchair and slid my body into the middle of the office floor, not caring who saw or who had to walk around me. Pain colored all my decisions.

I got the injection, but in the end, the shot did nothing to dull my aching discomfort.

That next night, in my Irish-Catholic-independent fashion, though I wasn't any better, I told Joanna to go home.

I knew I was lucky to have friends and neighbors where all I had to do was ask, and they would be there for me. But at this moment, I just wanted to hide. I'm not sure why I wanted this, but it felt natural to me. Part of me thought, "*I am strong enough to do this on my own.*" While another part wondered, "*Do I just not want these close friends to see me so weak, to see me cry? Am I too scared to accept help because that would be acknowledging I need it, that I'm not 'independent and I can no longer take care of myself?*"

For the next few nights, my "me-time" was reduced to simply lying face down in my bed, staring at the underarm of my bicep. This was the only position that was remotely comfortable. I just laid there, staring and praying.

I was born and bred Catholic. My parents were

committed Catholics and made sure their children went to Catholic schools for the best education they could dream of. On top of that, I grew up with my Uncle Bernard, a priest, and an aunt, Sister Michele Doyle, who is in the order of the School Sisters of Saint Francis. My mom used to say, "I have a sister who is a nun, a brother who was a priest, and I married a saint." I loved my heritage, but as I grew up and began to have my own opinions, the workings of the Vatican began to bug the hell out of me. I couldn't understand why they just didn't sell part of Michelangelo's work and feed the poor. What was with all this high and mighty BS?

Whenever I would come to my mom and complain about the latest statement a Pope[1] made that I disagreed with, she would say, "Don't worry about those men in Rome. Pray to Mary!"

Through the years, I had taken Mom's advice and began to have a special affinity for Mary. So as I laid in bed, feeling basically paralyzed, I prayed to Mary over and over again. *Mary, please take the agony away. Mary, please give me hope for an answer. Mary, please give me my life back.*

I bargained with God, offering up promises of being a better person and not ever taking my health for granted again. In my weakness, I may have bartered that I'd become a nun if my suffering would go away.[2] As soon as I said that I knew God was probably thinking, "Pick another promise, Pat."

As I prayed over and over again, I thought of the football version of a "Hail Mary," where with time expiring on the

1. Not this current Pope. I love Pope Francis because he actually puts his feet in the shoes of others.
2. As a young girl, I loved *The Flying Nun*, and my family thought I would become a nun, but that ship has long sailed out to sea.

game clock, the quarterback launches a desperate ball into the endzone in the hopes that a miracle might happen and a teammate will catch the ball for the game winning touchdown. Just like a quarterback knows his best receiver can find a way to make that remarkable catch, I knew Mary could hear my prayers. Thus, for a week I stayed up all night, praying the traditional Hail Mary Catholic prayer. One night, I counted as I said one thousand Hail Marys, hoping that I too might make a last-minute, game-ending miracle happen.

For my non-Catholic readers, the Hail Mary prayer goes like this:

Hail Mary,
Full of Grace,
The Lord is with thee.
Blessed art thou among women,
and blessed is the fruit
of thy womb, Jesus.
Holy Mary,
Mother of God,
pray for us sinners now,
and at the hour of our death.

Amen.

As the days rolled one into the other, I wasn't seeing a miracle (not to say one wasn't developing beyond my peripheral vision). I was in more agony than I'd ever experienced, but I kept telling concerned friends that I was fine. I'm not sure if it was my pride or sturdy Midwestern roots, but I believed I could ride out this storm alone.

At the end of that first week, Marty took me to an orthopedic surgeon.

"You'll tell us when you're ready," the surgeon said. I didn't understand it at the time, but back surgery is almost always elective and driven by the patient's pain. When the pain becomes too much, patients turn toward back surgery, which is risky and requires a long road of recovery.

Again, sitting in the wheelchair intensified my discomfort, so I slid to the office lobby floor. My suffering was so intense that I was shrieking and crying inconsolably on the ground.

Unbeknownst to Marty and me, the surgeon and nurses were saying, "She's not going to last the night."

I lasted the night. A thousand more Hail Marys.

The next morning, my neighbor, Cathy, sent me a text saying she wanted to bring me coffee and asked how I was doing.

I texted back: "*Not good.*"

This was one of the first times in my life that I'd put up the white flag of surrender. There was no way I was going to be able to do this alone. Cathy and my other neighbors, Marie, Cindy, and Cynthia, rushed over, and soon I had a house full of neighbors at my side, problem-solving, rubbing my feet, talking to potential doctors, and caring for me. These people had been my neighbors for more than twenty years, and they were my team! But it was clear to them that I had to go to the ER again.

Eventually, Marty and a couple of the men in my neighborhood carried me out of my home to get into Marty's car again. As I looked at my neighbors, my friends, tears were filling their eyes. They had never seen me like this. I was the one working in the yard, hauling mulch, and mowing my lawn every weekend with the rest of them. I was strong, able, and a master of my own fate. *This wasn't me.*

I didn't know it then as I took in their faces, but my life had been forever altered. One moment I was flying high after a golf cart ride, and in an instant, my hopes and dreams fell mid-flight. I would've never guessed that only days later I would soon be heading to two hospitals and a rehabilitation center, and I wouldn't see my home for weeks.

Hope Nugget: Hold up that white flag of surrender proudly. We can only overcome our biggest trials by having people by our side.

Chapter 2

An Encounter With Hope

After a few nights in the ER, I was admitted to the main hospital where the doctors toyed with what to do with me. They finally came to the conclusion that the thing I probably needed was a spinal fusion surgery, but their surgeons would not have any openings to do the surgery for at least a few weeks. They informed me that I would stay in the hospital another night, but then would be transported to a rehabilitation center the next day until a surgery slot opened up. Though this was the only option they were giving me, I still had to make the decision whether or not to do it. I felt like I needed more information. In fact, I still wasn't sure what exactly had happened to me, except that something had come undone in my back.

I knew a couple of friends who had a similar surgery before. I called them up, but both friends told me that the surgery had been terrible for them. Not exactly what I wanted to hear, but at least they were honest. I then Googled the surgery, but there was so much mixed information that it was overwhelming to try and come up with a pros and cons list. I began wishing that I had a partner to advocate for me in all this. It became so hard to focus and feel confidence in my judgment while on pain medication, and it terrified me. I was spiraling into a blur of uncertainty and discouragement, when the PA on duty entered my room with a smile on her face.

"Pat, I have good news! A cancellation occurred tomorrow, which means a surgery opened up for you if you want it!"

"Oh wow." I wasn't sure how to process this information aside from my eyes welling with tears.

"Pat, what's wrong?"

"I'm just really confused on if I should do this or not. What do you think?"

"Pat, your back is broken. It needs to be fixed. These are great surgeons. I think you should do it."

Her assurance gave me a peace I hadn't yet felt in this mess, and I decided she was right.

"Okay, I'll do it."

The team began to prepare me for surgery, which sadly meant no food or drink for the rest of the day. I did my best to sleep that night, still nervous, but praying my Hail Mary's, and hoping that this was the right choice, hoping this was all I needed to get back to my life.

The next morning a doctor came in and told me I was being moved to a rehabilitation center.

"No. I'm supposed to have surgery this morning!"

"No, you're not. There is no record of that on my clipboard."

"The PA told me yesterday that you had a cancellation and we decided I would take the opening. They've been prepping me for surgery the last twenty-four hours."

"I'm telling you, it's not on my schedule. We are sending you to a rehab facility. Sometimes with this you can do a minimally invasive procedure. An opening for that should pop up sooner than a fusion."

Then he abruptly left the room. And I lost it. I was having a nervous breakdown and could barely breathe. *This can't be happening to me!*

Thankfully, my breakdown was interrupted by my friend Alissa who was at the hospital visiting another friend and had heard I was there. She came into my room, listened, and consoled me. Then she sprung to action, grabbing the dry erase marker the nurses used on the whiteboard with my patient information on it. With a glint in her eye, she said, "Pat, we are going to make some goals! What do you want to do when you get out of here?"

My first response was, "To get back to my life."

Alissa wrote that on the board, and then asked, "Okay, what does that look like?"

"To play tennis." She scribbled this on the board.

"To do the Colin's Hope swim again." She smiled as she wrote that down. Alissa was the Executive Director of Colin's Hope—a non-profit dedicated to preventing drowning accidents. One of their annual fundraisers was an open water swim event, which I always loved to participate in and support.

"Okay, give me one more, Pat!"

"To do a triathlon." She put that down too.

"See Pat this isn't the end of your story. You are going to get out of here soon and be able to do these things again."

Before she left, she gave me a gift. It was a shirt that said, *Trust the Process.* As I held it in my hands, I allowed myself to take a long, deep breath for the first time in days. Perhaps

God had better plans for me than a rushed surgery. *Just trust the process, Pat.*

Later the hospital sent me on my way to the rehabilitation center. I was put into a tin can of an ambulance where every bump and use of the brake hurt me to the core. One driver was focused on the road, and the other paramedic was occupied with texting on his phone—I'm sure he was on Tinder trying to find a date—and I hated that not only was he doing nothing to make the ride more comfortable, but he also wasn't asking for my opinion on potential life partners for him. The ride was torturous, and when I arrived at the rehab center, I was in agony. I started telling the attendants what to do and how to take care of me. It wasn't pretty. It was early evening, and after what felt like forever, they finally got me settled into a room and on drugs to ease the pain.

I woke up the next morning at five a.m., confused and angry. *Why am I here?* These had been the absolute worst days of my life, and I was assured that I did not belong in such a dismal place. I quickly observed other people in the center and came to the conclusion that I was right. I could not belong in the same place where I only saw the elderly or the extremely put out. This had to be a mistake. Didn't they know how capable I was? Sure I was in pain, but I was confident that I could take care of myself. I needed answers. I needed to prove I could find a way to move on my own. I couldn't stay here. I was afraid that if I did, I would lose my independence for good. That wasn't me. Thus, I had one goal: I needed to be home.

I had no idea where I was in the therapy center, but I wanted out. I knew I was only a couple of miles away from home, and I decided I would walk home. I pulled out all the

IVs and monitors on me. I saw there was a walker near my bed, which was just the tool I needed.

I had never used a walker and could barely feel or move my left leg, but I somehow used it to hobble down the hall. From what I could see, my room was at the end of the hallway, and as I looked around, I saw no nurses, doctors, or physical therapists. It was eerily quiet, and as I struggled walking down the hall, I noticed all the doors were closed. I was looking for a way out when I saw at the end of the hallway a patient's door open with the curtain pulled back.

I peered in and saw the most beautiful older woman with striking blue eyes reaching out to me with her hand. I felt drawn to her, compelled to grab her hand and look into those piercing eyes.

"What's your name?" I asked.

"Hope."

I'm sure my face and mouth dropped to the floor. I realized I had lost hope and was running away. I'd forgotten to have faith now that I knew surgeries could be on the horizon and that my life was about to change. Meeting Hope, the woman, gave me the strength to stay at the rehab facility. We visited every day I was there, and our little chats gave me just the boost to believe better days would come again. I found out she was ninety-six years old and had broken her hip. We raised each other up and would wave from across the rehab room. I was in pain and had no clear vision for my future, but for the first time since I'd walked into my house and collapsed in pain, I thought that maybe I could heal. It was just a small taste of optimism, but it filled my soul.

The lesson Hope taught me is that we all need a connection, and never more so than when we're in pain and in a strange place. I thought I should be running home (well, dragging my left leg and staggering home), but honestly, I was lonely and just needed a connection. Hope made me feel less isolated and reminded me that we all need to have a sense of belonging no matter where we are. Hope with her beautiful, inspiring name and lovely nature was a reminder from the Universe or my guardian angels that a bigger plan was in play, and that I should do my best to have the faith and patience to see it out. So I stayed put.

I look like a ghost of myself, I thought as I glanced at myself in the mirror of the rehab center bathroom I was in.

It had been two weeks of being in and out of the hospital and the rehabilitation center, and I didn't recognize myself. In only two weeks, I felt like my muscles were completely gone, and as I looked at myself in the mirror, I could see that the definition in my arms and legs was waning. I hadn't been able to move, let alone work out, play tennis, or do yard work in two freaking weeks! I 'couldn't remember the last time I didn't work out for two days, let alone two weeks.

I shook my head, hoping that would erase these thoughts from my brain.

"Freaking *patrophy*," I said out loud to myself. It took me a moment before I realized I had changed atrophy to *patrophy*. I laughed at that one, and it felt good. If anything, this situation was giving me more insight and compassion for others, proving just how grateful I was for the life I usually lived. I would do anything to get back to that life. First though, I needed answers.

After a fortnight of suffering, the orthopedic surgeon came in and announced the news, "Your MRI shows that you've ruptured multiple disks in your back, and your lumbar has shifted from your spine. It looks like this was caused by a condition known as spondylolisthesis, which you must've had for a time. Spondylolisthesis is where your vertebrae begin to break down and slip. The vertebrae in your lumbar have been slipping and now are so far out of place that they have been pressing on your discs, causing that rupture in your low back, and are currently pressing on your nerves causing your severe back and leg pain."

I finally had the official answer (well, *answers*). It was the pressure on my nerves and discs, and the separation of my lumbar from my spine causing the excruciating back pain and throbbing agony in my left leg. There was no way to know for sure how the spondylolisthesis had developed. It could either be genetic, or something developed by a tweak or accident, especially in athletes as they aged. I learned it was fairly common to live your life not knowing you had the condition because the symptoms didn't always present them-selves until they were extreme. In reflection, my back had been sore here and there, but I just figured everyone had back pain as they aged, and it was nothing serious. Appar-ently, I was wrong. I was told surgery was needed and I chose to begin with the minimally invasive option, fully hopeful that it would solve my problems. *This will fix it all.*

I was optimistic that opting in for the minimally invasive surgery would mean I could skip "The Big Kahuna"— the name I'd given to the bigger, multi-level spinal fusion surgery with the titanium rods and screws that would be needed to restabilize my spine permanently. The Big Kahuna is always a last resort, and the more I read about it online, the more horror stories I was exposed to about the tough recovery and slim chances of returning to an active lifestyle.

The surgeon was skeptical. "Hey, you can try the less invasive surgery, but no promises. You may still need the fusion after this."

I put up a brave face and acted confident in my choice in front of the surgeon, but after my decision, I second guessed everything. I was driving around town being stubborn and staying off pain pills to be as independent as possible. As I kept researching my next steps, my head was spinning, and I wondered if I was doing the right thing. *Has pain clouded my judgment? Am I making the right decision to have surgery? Would I ever be pain-free again and return to my life?* I wanted to believe I could be one of the lucky ones. I was both looking forward to and dreading the upcoming surgery.

To calm my nerves, I ended up visiting my general practitioner, Dr. Casey Clor. I was lying down in his office because I couldn't sit, as we discussed the pros and cons of surgery. It was at that moment Dr. Clor gave me the most precious gift. He squeezed my hand, and said, "Pat, there are going to be good days and bad days, and I'm here to tell you, I'm in it with you. I'll be here for all the days."

Dr. Clor's simple declaration of support lifted my spirits. I trusted his guidance and expertise, but it was the human touch and empathy that filled me with relief. I wish more doctors knew that hope and compassion are two of the most powerful healing treatments.

On May 15, 2018, I had a lumbar disc microsurgery where my surgeon removed my ruptured disk matter. As the anesthesia wore off and the surgeon came into my room to tell me the results of my surgery, he told me, "I've been doing this surgery for a long time. You had the largest chunk of disc matter that I've ever taken out."

I'd later find out that he saved my massive disc matter as an example for medical students and other surgeons. I chalk it up to living in Texas, where we go big or go home.

Despite all my positive affirmations about returning to my active life, I didn't feel much better after the surgery. I was in constant pain with nerves frequently misfiring. I felt tiny bouts of progress, but not the miracle I needed to restart living my best life.

Work kept continuing on though and even with pain as my constant companion, I wanted to prove to my job that I was okay. At the time, I was a leader in sales training in the diamond industry. I was the Vice President of Learning and Development for a large luxury diamond brand. I did workshops all over the world, and loved using storytelling to help retail jewelers and sales associates find the inspiration to sell diamonds emotionally, making a connection with their customers.

I would tell them how my proudest diamond sales were the sales where the customer never even saw the diamond before purchasing it. I was able to describe the diamond I wanted them to buy without them seeing it. I wouldn't describe what we call the 4C's in the diamond industry (cut, color, clarity, carat weight). Instead, I'd describe what the diamond would do for them. *It will sparkle, dance, and act like a camera flash in a dark room. When it gets darker the diamond will be brighter. People will compliment you on how beautiful it is.*

Once I sold the diamond, I would hang up the phone and start doing my "diamond dance" and my colleague Mike would laugh and congratulate me. He knew what the "diamond dance" meant. He would smile and give me a thumbs up. I learned that it's not the technical details that make a sale. It's in the beauty. It's in what the product or service will do for your customer. A successful person will not sell the product, they will sell the need. I wanted sales associates to know that they are forever a part of people's stories, and to realize the significance of that.

"Do you really know why someone comes in to buy their significant other a diamond? Unveiling the hidden reason why is one of the most beautiful parts of our jobs. Most of the time, I've discovered that the person buying their significant other a diamond has this unspoken desire to be a hero. A guy wowing his girlfriend makes him feel like he is doing it right."

Our career was rewarding, but no story I could tell would ever compare to the story of my dad buying a diamond from me. My parents had been married for fifty years, and the only piece of jewelry my dad had bought my mom was her engagement ring.

One day he called me up and wanted me to help him buy my mom a diamond pendant for Christmas.

"Dad, are you sick? Are you dying?" Never in my twenty-five years of working in the diamond industry had he ever approached me about buying my mom a diamond.

"No, no, nothing like that! But it's time. I want to give her a really nice diamond pendant." He knew the exact style of pendant he wanted and together we found the right one for mom. We created an 18-karat yellow gold custom pendant complete with a one carat brilliant round diamond with an excellent cut, polish, and symmetry.

Christmas morning came and when my mom opened the present from my dad she was completely stunned. She immediately put it on (and has never taken it off since), her face beaming beyond belief.

A couple of weeks later, my dad called me up again. "Pat, I want to give your mom another diamond."

"Whoa but, Dad, you just gave her an amazing diamond pendant."

"I know, but I want to give her something for our anniversary in February. I'm thinking of an anniversary band of diamonds."

"All right, Dad. We can work on this, but I'm curious. Why do you want to give her another big gift, something so important, so close together?"

"Pat, if I would've known how that pendant would make her feel, I would've been giving her diamonds a long time ago."

At the end of this story, I always loved to show two pictures of my parents. The first picture is at Christmas right after she opens the pendant. My mom is displaying a big, shocked look while my dad has a contented smile on his face. He knows he did good.

But in the second photo, the grin I can't stop looking at is the giant one on my dad's face as he gets ready to give Mom the diamond band, waiting in giddy anticipation for my mother's reaction on their anniversary. More than the gift itself is that he knows how this gift is going to make my mom feel, and that's everything. This is why jewelers do what we do.

I loved my job.

I traveled all over the world for my job. I got to crawl down diamond mines in South Africa and stood on ships watching diamonds being mined off the shores of Namibia. Seeing the journey of a natural diamond forming reminded me how the fires we are going through can actually be creating our most powerful selves. I learned how diamonds can be a powerful gift to a country's development with fair trade agreements and impactful social and environmental programs that transform lives.

On one such trip to South Africa, I decided to make it an extended stay and go on a safari. I wanted to go to the most untouched jungles, and thus signed up to go to the Okavango Delta in Botswana. I couldn't find a friend to go with me, so I decided to hire a guide and launch out alone.

My guide and I started in Zimbabwe, and we drove through a jungle for hours. It was extremely hot—our Jeep didn't have air conditioning—and my guide was driving with the

windows rolled up. He didn't smell all too pleasant and after a while, neither did I. But he never rolled down the windows. Eventually, I couldn't stand it anymore, so I rolled down my window and tried to go to sleep—not an easy task on the extremely bumpy road we were on. Somehow, I fell asleep. I wasn't sure how long I'd been out, but when I woke up, I looked down at my T-shirt and was shocked to see that I was covered in blood. I thought I had been shot there was so much blood. After catching my breath, I noticed a crap ton of tiny flies everywhere—tsetse flies. They had been biting me and drawing blood while I slept. Now I knew why my guide had kept the windows rolled up. I should have followed his lead.

A few hours later, I'd forgotten that lesson and had to learn it all over again. And this

time, the experience was even scarier. When we got to the border with Botswana we stopped. There was no checkpoint, no border security, nothing. My guide—whose name, believe it or not, was Thinkwell—got out of the Jeep and pulled out his passport. And then he did something really weird. He stood on a log, held up his passport in the air and waved it around while shout-counting to ten in his native language.

When he had finished counting, he came back to the Jeep and told me to do the same

thing. I couldn't believe this.

"No way! You're just playing a trick on me so you can laugh at me," I said with a wink.

"No," Thinkwell replied somberly. "You have to do it. We can't go any farther until you

stand on the log, hold up your passport, and count to ten."

My dumb self wouldn't budge, and thus, we went back and forth on this for a few minutes. When he wouldn't let it go, finally I decided what does it hurt to humor him?

I got out of the Jeep, stepped on the log, held up my passport, and started counting.

By the time I got to number five, I looked up and fear overtook me when I realized what was happening. Up in the trees, not ten feet away, were four men with machine guns pointing directly at me. Apparently, this was the border patrol for Botswana. I continued counting as they stared me down until finally, Thinkwell said it was okay to come back to the Jeep. Apparently, we passed the test and the men with machine guns thought we were okay enough to let through.

I was pretty shaken up by this encounter and didn't question Thinkwell again. When we got to the Okavango Delta, I realized it was all worth it. My reward was to see elephants and giraffes, lions and hippos, rhinos and zebras in their natural habitat. I was overwhelmed with wonder and had to pinch myself while thinking, *How did I get here? This is too remarkable!*

The week of July 16, I wanted to prove to my company that I could travel and get back on the horse after my first surgery. I had to use a cane, which I hated, but I did it. At the end of a busy week of training and multi-city visits though, I was brought into my corporate office.

"I'm sorry, Pat, but we've eliminated your position," my boss said.

What? I thought I had blacked out for a moment until I saw the nervous expression on my boss' face and knew I had heard her correctly. I was crushed. With this out-of-the-blue decision, I felt my entire world crumbling beneath me. *What's next? How much more can I handle? Why is everything falling apart at once?*

It was a long four-hour flight home.

A few days later, I still couldn't feel my leg or walk. On July 23rd, I went back to the surgeon wondering why my leg still felt ready to blow, inquiring how much longer it would be until I was back on the tennis court or out running.

"Hey, my leg doesn't feel better. I'm walking with two canes. It feels like I'm being stabbed all-day long."

These nerve pain "zingers" would come out of nowhere with a painful electric shock. When the zinger would hit, I'd scream or tumble or fall. The pain was so intense that I couldn't stop the ear-splitting sounds that came from my body. I would scream or cry out involuntarily, and it was happening all the time.

"I'm sorry. Sometimes these things work, and sometimes they don't. If you want to get back to your life and be active, you're going to have to do the 2 Level fusion," my surgeon said nonchalantly as if this next step wasn't a big deal. The surgery would use titanium rods and screws to fuse my lumbar and spine back together. This was *The Big Kahuna.*

I was shocked, and not prepared at all for that response. I was expecting to hear, "give it a little more time, be patient, you'll be better soon." Instead, I was crestfallen. I had put so much hope into the minimally invasive surgery and the rehab that followed. I left the surgeon's office feeling alone and defeated. It was time for the Big Kahuna surgery, and I was despondent, utterly devoid of optimism.

I went home feeling so sorry for myself and so alone, when I got a text from some of my tennis team friends.

We're going to happy hour. Meet us!

Here I was, having another one of the worst days of my life. The surgery would take two years to recover from—if it worked—and there was so much conflicting advice on the internet. It was a big, scary surgery, and I was terrified to face it.

But something about that text moved me. *I could give up or try and have a life in the middle of this pain and uncertainty.* So I headed to one of my favorite spots at a marina near my home and had two large glasses of chardonnay with my caring friends. I hadn't been eating much over the last month, so I felt the alcohol come on strong.

I was in a terrible mindset and so distraught that after the second glass I couldn't fake it any longer. I was feeling worse than I had before I came. *Why did I come at all?* I couldn't pretend anymore so I apologized to my friends and headed back to my car.

As I entered the parking lot to make my way home, I saw a man walking his two dogs. There was a beautiful, big white labrador and a cute, feisty dachshund making a beeline straight toward me. Dogs, kids, and drunks have *always* been attracted to me. If I'm at a party and there's a dog, it's right by my side. I'm that person, and luckily I love animals and kids (but I could do without the drunks).

As the man got closer, the two dogs pulled harder on their leashes, trying to reach me. When the big white lab finally got to me, I leaned down to pet him. In his excitement (and maybe because of the two chardonnays), our timing was off, and as I bent to pet him, he head-butted me in the mouth. He was so strong that our face bump made my two front teeth cut through my lip.

In an instant, I started to bleed inside my mouth, and my face and lip were swelling up. *Really, God, you're going to take my two front teeth and put them through my lip. Today?*

I could taste blood and see it dripping off my chin. I didn't want any help, and I didn't want the dogs' owner to feel bad for what had been an accident. So, I tried to hide my bleeding face by leaning down to pet the smaller dachshund.

"What's the dachshund's name?"

"Hope."

I literally guffawed. "It's not Hope. Are you serious? Is it really Hope?"

I'm sure this man thought I was crazy by making such a big deal of his dog's name, but it was just the sign I needed. Screw the blood and fat lip; I had literally been struck in the face with Hope! I took a picture of Hope the dog because I couldn't believe it. It had been a horrible day, but even with my swollen, bloody lip, I had found hope again.

Hope Nugget: Don't be afraid to open your eyes to the signs of hope all around you. They're often in the most unexpected places.

Chapter 3

The Big Kahuna

I had heard horror stories from friends that warned that the Big Kahuna surgery was to be avoided at all costs. Looking up 2 Level fusions on the internet was terrifying as all the news was extremely negative about fusions. Beware of the internet—it can lead you down some dark paths. I saw numerous posts of people saying the surgery was the worst pain of their lives, that the recovery was difficult, and that many people felt *worse* after the surgery. I heard other stories though, where people did get better after the surgery. The more research I did, the more I realized that everybody's back surgery was different. I had to focus on what was right for me.

I was so unhappy and riddled with pain, I decided to take the leap forward and do the 2 Level fusion. My fears were overcome with this persistent piece of courage that wanted to believe I could get back to where I was. I hoped the surgery would be that difficult steppingstone that would be worth it to live pain free again.

The thing was I did have options as to where I could

have this surgery done. I wanted to find a surgeon who I trusted in a hospital that I was confident in, and I had just the place in mind.

Growing up in Iowa, the Mayo Clinic in Rochester, Minnesota was always this enchanting place three hours north from us. The Mayo Clinic had a stellar reputation for cutting-edge medicine and having an amazing staff. Mayo was also notorious for treating some of the most incredible historical figures of our time from former presidents to Helen Keller to June and Johnny Cash, Ernest Hemingway, Lou Gehrig, and even the Dalai Lama. Most importantly, my dad was one of their patients back in 2010 when he underwent back surgery, and I remember it being a unique and beautiful experience.

This hospital had a philosophy I call "The Mayo Way" that seeped compassion, patience, and excellence into every employee that worked there, which I believe started in its origins. Mayo had developed out of a small family practice in Rochester where Dr. William Mayo practiced medicine with his two sons—Dr. Will and Dr. Charlie. When a tornado wreaked havoc in their town in 1883, the Mayos put it upon themselves to oversee recovery efforts partnering with the nearby convent of the Sisters of Saint Francis. It was early on in this partnership that Mother Alfred Moes, the leader of the convent, told Dr. Mayo God had given her a vision to build a hospital and to appoint Dr. Mayo as the director. To this day, there is something about Mayo that still feels like a small family practice partnering with the divine compassion of a group of Sisters. It had been three months since collapsing in my home, and I knew on a gut-level that Mayo was where I was supposed to be.

By the time my case was accepted by Mayo, and I could

schedule a consultation, it was November 2018. I flew to Rochester, Minnesota, for a consultation visit at Mayo. Even though I knew the decision to do the spinal fusion and do it at the world-renowned Mayo Clinic were the right choices, I was still terrified.

The minute I stepped off the plane in Rochester though, I felt this immediate compassion from everyone that worked there. The airport employees were all super friendly and kept things light-hearted because they knew everyone who went to Mayo was dealing with something serious. I realized then that "Minnesota nice" is a real thing.

I remember lots of smiles and being asked, "You here for Mayo? It's the best! Good luck." The airport personnel offered to carry my bags and helped me find the shuttle for the Marriott SpringHill Suites in Rochester, where Mayo Clinic patients and family often stayed. Mom had made the three-hour drive to stay with me in the hotel and support me through all my appointments the next day.

I didn't feel the full impact the toll waiting for the spinal fusion had on me until I walked into the lobby of the Gonda Building at the Mayo Clinic for the first time. There was a huge, multi-floor open space where I saw people of all nationalities and types of clothing queuing in line. There were men in suits and other men in overalls. There were women adorned with headscarves and others wearing trucker hats. City slickers and rural folks. Athletes and artists. The elderly and the young.

I had noticed license plates in the parking lot from all over the country, and this checked out with the different accents I heard utterances of. A little Mississippi drawl here, a little Minnesotan cadence there, and even some surfer bro inflection, which stereotypically made me think of California. There seemed to be no algorithm to the type of person receiving treatment at Mayo, and that fact encouraged my feeling of belonging. I was overwhelmed by the sheer heart of this place. It was what I imagined peace looked like in physical form.

People moved in and out of the lobby, some at a rapid pace, while others moved at the more leisurely pace their body allowed. Some were in wheelchairs—I couldn't help but watch a woman, who only had half her skull, be pushed tenderly in her wheelchair by her adoring husband. Some were walking with canes. Some limped without assistance. Others walked normally and I didn't have any idea what their ailment was. I witnessed a gorgeous, six-foot-tall woman running sprints in a hallway with a prosthetic leg. She was so fit that I knew she had to be some kind of Olympian. The thing all these souls had in common though was everyone was with someone. As that fact hit, I couldn't be more grateful that my mom was there with me. It was difficult for me to know that I, a fifty-six-year-old woman, was being supported by her eighty-six-year-old mother, but now I know it was the silver lining in all this. It was a gift. I was the luckiest person in the world at that moment.

There were large, floor-to-ceiling windows letting in the winter sunlight, smooth, polished woods, and beautiful marble touches everywhere. It was stunning. This was where patients checked in, and it was as organized as a five-star Vegas hotel.

As I was about to make my way to the check-in desk, I was stopped in my tracks by the most beautiful music being played on a gorgeous piano in the center of the lobby. As my ears took in the classical melody, I had this overwhelming feeling that I was in a place of healing, a place that cared about me. I felt like I'd arrived somewhere holy, and all of the stress, pain, and confusion of the last nine months washed away. The music touched my soul, and my face was wet with tears after only a few minutes of listening. This was the moment I had been waiting for after all the sleepless nights and thousands of Hail Mary prayers I'd been uttering day after day.

I could feel the energy and the unity in this space. We were all looking for answers to whatever illness plagued us, and we were here because we were persistent. When other doctors had told us they didn't know what was wrong with us, we knew deep down there was still hope somewhere. This feeling both saddened and comforted me. There were countless others in as bad of shape, or much worse than I. All of these people had their life disrupted by their body betraying them, and yet science and the medical field had come so far that it could easily be mistaken for wizardry.

"This must be the most magical place on earth," I thought to myself. Of course, I'd never been to Disney World, so the jury was still out on that one.

I learned on my first consultation that Mayo worked in teams. *"Teamwork"* wasn't just a platitude mounted on an inspirational poster, but the cornerstone of how Mayo practiced medicine. Neurologists, orthopedic surgeons, physical therapists, and nurses worked in tandem. That approach was different from what I had experienced in Austin. All of my doctors had been skilled and caring, but I felt as if I was alone and the only one making sure that everything worked together. At Mayo, that burden was lifted.

My surgeon was Dr. Paul Huddleston, and I came to think of him as our team coach. He was honest and caring, and I felt something uniquely different about Mayo Clinic and Dr. Huddleston. On this first in-person visit, I brought with me an 8x10 photo of me with a group of badass women right after we finished a triathlon. In the photo, I'm beaming as I look healthy, strong, fit, and radiant. *Yep, that is who I am.*

I told Dr. Huddleston, "What you see in front of you isn't who I am. It isn't." Then I handed the picture over to him. "*This* is who I am. I need to get back to that person."

Dr. Huddleston looked me straight in the eyes and responded, "Pat, there's hope. This is a hopeful situation. We will fix this."

My biggest fear had been that he would tell me he couldn't do anything for me—that I'd have to live every day in unrelenting pain. To hear that he believed this would work and he wasn't giving up on me made me feel like I was part of this team. I wouldn't be left to fight the problem on my own, and his words flooded my body with gratitude. I was still nervous about the two-level spinal fusion surgery where the surgeon would use titanium rods and screws to restabilize my spine permanently, using some of my own bone marrow to rebuild my discs, but I knew I had the right team behind me.

After a few pre-op meetings, we scheduled the spinal fusion for January 4th, 2019. It was a little wild to schedule surgery in January in the frozen tundra that would be Rochester,

Minnesota, but I was sure that the sooner I did this, the sooner I would be back to my old life.

I stayed with Mom in Des Moines and visited with my family through Thanksgiving and Christmas. The plan was that I'd also stay with Mom after the surgery until I was well enough to move back to Austin.

On January 2nd, Mom and I drove up to Rochester. We stayed at the same Marriot as before and enjoyed the in-room coffee maker and a small fridge to keep food cold. The last thing on either of our minds was food, so we'd just have bed picnics with PB&J sandwiches. We both enjoyed quiet and I loved the low-key nature of staying together. We didn't need a whole lot and just passed the time by talking and laughing.

On January 4th, the day of surgery, I was up at four a.m. Mom had wanted to come, but Mayo didn't allow anyone in the pre-op room, so I made her stay. The hotel was just a few blocks away from St. Mary's Campus—the part of Mayo where the big surgeries take place. St. Mary's was started by a group of nuns known as the Sisters of Saint Francis who later partnered with the Mayo brothers to create the incredible medical facility it is today. After the thousands of Hail Mary's I had prayed over the past few months, I thought this was a very appropriate name for the building I would have my surgery in.

I relished the idea of walking there—walking toward the new me. It didn't matter that it was only five degrees Fahrenheit outside. I was ready. I put on my huge, white parka, placed headphones in my ears and cranked up my favorite playlist.

As I left the hotel room, the first song that came on was the "Theme for Rocky." I turned the music up as loud as my ears could handle. It was dark, and the chilly air was pelting me like gunfire, but I loved it. I imagined I was running up those famous Philadelphia steps with Rocky by my side. Each step I took was like another round withstanding the blows from heavyweight champ Apollo Creed. I was going to persevere like never before. I was going to get my life back.

Before I knew it, I'd made it to St. Mary's Campus. As I walked through the hospital doors, I almost expected an entire crowd to be cheering for me and my performance. Instead, I was instantly rolled into surgery. The room was overwhelming, with more people than I could count hurriedly working around me with a huge white light above. Alone on the operating table, I began to cry. Part of that was fear—all these strangers ready to cut me open. I'd heard so many stories about the horrors of this surgery. The success rate wasn't in my favor. One-third of patients felt the same, one-third of patients were worse, and a last lucky third improved. The other catalyst was relief. After months and months of searching for anything that could be recognized as a solution, here I was. I had *finally* made it.

One of the nurses leaned next to me right when I was about to go under and held my hand saying, "What's wrong? You're going to be fine."

"I've waited so long. I'm no longer scared. But to finally be here, heading to surgery, I'm so ready to get this over with!" I was full on bawling now.

"Don't worry, hon. You're in good hands."

"I feel like such a baby."

"Everybody cries," she remarked soothingly.

Before the surgery, I had watched a lot of *Grey's Anatomy* and knew that surgeons played music while they worked. I asked one of the nurses, "Will you play 50 Cent's 'In Da Club (It's Your Birthday)'? It's my birthday in a couple of weeks, and I know I will still be in the hospital then."

"Sure, hon," she replied.

They started to play the song and I could hear the first few beats of the song followed by an eruption of giggles. I smiled, and that's the last thing I remembered before I was fully out.

The first few days after the surgery were a blur. I was told the eight-and-a-half-hour surgery went well, but I was on strong pain medication that made me feel loopy and outside of time and space. Two nurses came into my room a couple days into my recovery and told me it was time for me to get up and try my first walk post-surgery. This seemed like the worst idea I'd ever heard of, but I was not one to back down from a challenge.

They helped me get out of my hospital bed at a glacial pace. I was so scared my body would cease up and not be able to move. As I stood, I began to get dizzy. The room was spinning, and I could vaguely make out the warped form of my mom in front of me.

"I'm going to be sick," I muttered.

"That's okay," my mom replied as she placed her arm on mine.

I met her words with projectile vomit, which splattered all over her freshly pressed blouse and perfect make-up. Mom always looked like an ad for Talbots, but I knew she had tried extra hard to look presentable because she had a crush on Dr. Huddleston and wanted to look her best for him. In fact, she always referred to him as Doctor Handsome to my sisters and me.

Even with all of that, this didn't faze her. She simply looked down at her blouse, and in her trademark Irish stoicism said, "Well, that wasn't the first time that happened." Despite everything, I started laughing. I couldn't believe I was laughing at a time like this, but my mom is just funny no matter what the circumstance is.

Once the dizziness subsided, a physical therapist came in and strapped me into a brace to give my back support as I learned how to use the walker they had set out for me. Slowly, I was led out to the hospital hallway to complete my first post-surgery walk. I was surrounded by vocals of encouragement, but I couldn't allow their words to land where I needed them to. Instead, I stayed in my own pain.

The physical therapist walked behind me, using his strength to keep me upright while my mom stood in front of me, taking one slow step backward at a time as I trudged along painfully. I felt like a toddler, taking their first steps. Except instead of looks of elation on the faces around me, I was met with intense looks of concern. Starting over isn't the same as the first time. It's often harder.

I was embarrassed to be so helpless and vulnerable. I didn't want eyes on me, I didn't want looks of pity, and I didn't want to appear weak. Thus, I walked with my head down. I told myself that if I kept my head down, no one would see me. This wasn't me, right?

I found out a couple days before surgery that Mayo had no private rooms and that I would be assigned a roommate. My immediate thought to this news was, *Hell no! I am* not *having a freaking roommate!* I'm a grown ass woman. I live alone. I don't do roommates. In fact, I *hate* roommates.

When I was in high school, I was assigned a roommate at the hotel we had to stay at for our big state swim meet. I did not want to share a room with someone I had never lived with. There were so many unknowns! When would she want to go to bed? What time would she wake up? Was she a nighttime shower-er or a morning shower-er? Would she snore? Would I feel comfortable enough to fall asleep? What if this threw off my routine the night before a big swim meet?

I decided it wasn't worth the risk, and snuck down to my parents' hotel room, where I felt more comfortable sleeping on their hotel room floor.

I had roommates in college—Yvonne and Teresa—and they were great. We got along well, which made it less difficult for me to share a room. Plus, college made it easier because we were always out doing activities and partying and only in our room to sleep. We partied, then slept. Or partied too late and didn't sleep. It worked!

The last time I'd actually had a roommate, I was in my early twenties working for my first big jewelry company and we had to room with someone for the sales convention. I hated it then too, but this time I had to suck it up as my parents weren't there to bail me out this time.

My friends all know: Pat doesn't do roommates. It had been over thirty years since I had a roommate in any capacity, and I was going to do everything in my power to keep it that way, especially at Mayo. I had absolutely no desire to go through what could be a traumatizing recovery process with a stranger sleeping in my room.

When I checked in at Mayo on the morning of the

surgery, I went up to the receptionist, and asked, "Now, can I pay a bit more money to not have a roommate?" She looked at me quizzically, probably wondering if I had hit my head and was confusing this hospital for the hotel I was staying at down the street.

"Yeah, no. You are definitely having a roommate," she firmly replied, squashing all ideas that Mayo was like a hotel where I could request the type of room I wanted. I'm pretty sure I growled inside my head.

Two days after surgery, I was stirred awake at three in the morning by nurses and doctors turning on my room lights, going in and out with supplies and charts, hurriedly apologizing to me. I realized this was the moment I had truly dreaded. This was the announcement that my roommate had arrived.

Before I could judge this roommate too harshly, I heard through the curtain dividing us a sweet older woman's voice, thick with a Minnesotan accent, constantly thanking the nurses as they assured her that she would be okay. It sounded like she had taken a nasty fall, which had brought her to the hospital. Poor thing.

After all the hustle and bustle, the medical staff left her alone. I'd overheard that she was scheduled for hip surgery in the morning, and I debated whether or not to say something to her. What was the protocol? Should I leave her alone and let her drift to sleep, or should I be a member of the welcome committee? As I debated my move, I heard her sweet voice, shakily asking me, "What's your name?"

"It's Pat."

"I'm Lucinda."

It started as simple as that, but we found pleasure in talking through the curtains. I learned she was eighty years

42

old and lived on a farm. Her husband had died years earlier, so she lived alone and had taken a fall that left her stranded in the cold on her front step for hours before someone found her. For a couple of days, we talked through the curtain. One night I threw up all night, and she reassured me. Then the next night, she was up vomiting all night, and I repaid the kindness.

Then a few days later, I went for my walk and finally saw Lucinda. She was the size of my pinky with skin that looked soft but weathered from years of farm labor. She had white hair with a darling curl to it that told me she was the kind of woman who wore rollers in her hair most nights. She was talking to her family and when she saw me walking by said, "I don't know why we need the curtain. We're good friends, we're close." And from then on, the curtain stayed open.

We had compassion for each other. Even though we were strangers, that connection and reassuring voice through the curtain was beyond healing. It reminded me to keep myself open for compassion, something we should all do. At that moment in my recovery, it felt good to do what I could to take care of everyone else. I was on the orthopedic floor where everyone was going through their own hell. There's always someone worse off than you are, and that's one of the biggest lessons I was learning at Mayo. To share your pain with others is a gift. To receive that empathy and also to give it back puts you on the best path for recovery.

When any of us are lonely, scared, or at a low point, we need to reach out. I learned that the nurses and doctors really want to know how we are doing, and turning to them for connection as a remedy for loneliness was a method of solace for me. From the staff that came in to clean my room to my physical therapist assisting me on my hallway walks, I began to form relationships, I began to know their stories, and it helped. People are the greatest asset we are gifted and leaning on them doesn't make one weak, but ushers in whispers of why we are here in the first place.

Hope Nugget: To share your pain with others is a gift. To receive that empathy and also to give it back puts you on the best path for recovery.

Chapter 4

Face the Storm Like an Eagle

"The Eagle does not escape the storm. The Eagle simply uses the storm to lift it higher. It spreads its mighty wings and rises on the winds that bring the storm."
—Jack White

I n my thirties, I remember sitting in an office in Boston being interviewed for a new global training position by the company's CEO. It was the type of interview where you had to solve a math formula on a chalkboard on the fly. There was a bombardment of intimidating questions that felt like walking through a minefield where one wrong answer could blow up in your face. I weaved and bobbed, handling this high-pressure interview as best I could.

Then the CEO asked, "What's your biggest fear?"

Without thinking or taking a breath, I answered, "That I won't be able to take care of myself and become a burden to my family and friends."

I could tell by the look on his face that I'd thrown him for a loop, and he was speechless. I guess most interviewers didn't say what truly frightened them in the dark of the night but couched their "fears" in something job-related. I thought my answer may have cost me the opportunity, but a few days later I found out I landed the job.

After three weeks at Mayo recovering from the Big Kahuna surgery, I was finally released and on my way to a rehab hospital near Mom's place in West Des Moines. I would be here a week or two for more acute recovery before being able to go home to Mom's for the next few months. Mom was driving me, and as I looked out the passenger side window, I couldn't help but think about that interview and wonder if my biggest fear was becoming my reality.

The truth was, I always feared being homeless and unable to take care of myself. I don't quite know where that fear came from, but there may be clues in how I was raised. I grew up in an Irish Catholic family in Urbandale, Iowa with my parents and two older sisters. We always had enough but nothing extra. We were not wealthy, but not poor either. We were a middle-class family where my parents always put their children's needs above their own, and waste was considered a sin. A common meal in our house was "Must Go," a term my mother used to describe leftovers where everything in the fridge must go. You name it (even SPAM) and it went on a piece of toast as a meal!

My parents opened a savings account for each of us by the time we were eight years old. Any time we got a card with money in it for a birthday or holiday, we would put it in our savings account. My parents had a motto they would remind us of with every dollar we were given: "Always save for a rainy day because you never know what might happen." I took this to heart and was thrilled with the rising amount of dollars that went into my savings each year.

My mom taught us to balance a checkbook (I wish I still did this, but I have a habit of thinking Wells Fargo is doing this for me). My dad encouraged us to never buy something on credit. If you can't afford it, don't buy it. To this day, I've never bought a car on credit.

Above all, we were loved and made the most of what we had. I never remember going without anything we truly needed. I was thankful and mostly happy about everything. I have fond memories of growing up and being among the first kids in line to see the latest Disney movie at the theater. After I purchased my ticket, I was beaming with excitement that I had a rare quarter left over for popcorn. Sometimes I would come home from school, and my mom would tell me there was a surprise waiting on my bed. I would rush upstairs to find a new pair of colorful underpants with flowers on them. When I told this story to a friend of mine, she remarked, "I would've gone up to my mom and asked, *Where the heck is the rest of the outfit?*"

I owned one or two pairs of shoes at a time, receiving new saddle shoes at the beginning of the school year to go with my uniform. It was important to my parents that their girls were dressed nicely. Along this theme, my dad came from a farming family where jeans were meant for workers and not something he wanted his teenage daughter wearing. In high school, I pleaded for a pair of Levi 501 jeans but didn't get a pair until I could buy them myself.

When that time came, I freaking loved the heck out of those jeans. They were the real thing, the kind of denim you have to wear for a few years to break in. Mine got so worn they became soft, and so torn that holes in the knees protruded through just like I hoped they would. I felt so cool every time I put these distressed jeans on. In due time though, there were a few holes that began to develop in the crotch area so one morning I was sewing those holes up when my sweet Grandma Doyle (my mom's mom) saw me and said, "Honey, if you need money for a new pair of pants, I can give you some."

"No thank you, Grandma. I'm good."

The next day, I was dismayed to find patches covering *all* the holes I worked so hard for. I knew this was the handiwork of Grandma Doyle who had made patches out of what looked like one of her old, flowery aprons. The only time I ever saw my Grandma Doyle without an apron on was at Catholic Mass. It took me all day to unstitch the patches.

A few weeks later, I ran down to her house on baking day, knowing she would give me some of her freshly baked bread. I lucked out and the bread was still warm when I got there. Score! I was wearing my jeans and when she saw my jeans with the knee holes back and open, she asked, "What happened to the patches?" When I tried to explain that I *wanted* some holes in my pants because it was the style, she looked at me as if I were an alien. That was the last time I talked to my grandma about fashion.

My other grandma, Catherine Henneberry, also had some quirks that have impacted my world view. She was an incredible athlete who was great at any sport she touched. She taught swimming lessons, and everyone admired her. I was often jealous of the kids she taught swimming to because I wanted such focused attention from her.

We would spend summers with extended family on my dad's side at a host of cabins in Saugatuck, Michigan—a little resort town on the eastern shore of Lake Michigan. Cousins, aunts, uncles, and, of course, grandparents were present. While in Saugatuck, I knew where to find my Grandma

Henneberry. She was most likely out swimming in the middle of the lake. She did long swimming workouts each day where she would swim out past the buoys, in rapid back and forth swim sprints. She had a beautiful side stroke and when she swam freestyle, it looked majestic. When I saw her out there, I would jump in and swim as fast as my little legs would let me until I was in the middle of the lake with her. This was my sacred alone time with her. This was how I got her attention. This is most likely why I fell in love with swimming.

The other memory I have of Grandma Henneberry is what she did when she took us kids out to a local diner for a meal. After she paid the bill, she would always take all the condiments on the table. Jelly, sugar, butter, salt, and pepper packets were emptied in her purse and then we would abruptly leave.

I remember one instance where the one waitress working must've been back in the kitchen and Grandma Henneberry hissed at me, "Pat, grab the ones from the other table!" I double checked that our waitress was nowhere in sight and grabbed the container holding the jelly packets, quickly sliding it to my grandma who dumped it into her purse and then immediately got up to leave.

This was a habit my grandma had formed having lived through the Great Depression. Though I was often embarrassed by the act, I knew I could always find sugar packets, jelly containers, or mints from restaurants in her purse. Us kids knew that if we ventured into Grandma's cabin, there would be toast and jelly waiting for us.

Another such tradition inspired by my Grandmother Doyle was that after dinner, our family would make tea. The unusual condition being that we shared one tea bag amongst all of us. It worked for us, and it wasn't until I was an adult making tea with a coworker where I grabbed her tea bag after she was done steeping and placed it in my own mug, that I discovered most people don't share tea bags. My coworker was disgusted and thought me very strange after that. Granted, I didn't care, and would still share a tea bag with one of my friends in a heartbeat.

In fact, on any given holiday, if you are at my mom's house, teabags are still shared to this day. It isn't unusual to see a teacup next to the sink with an old teabag in it just waiting for a fresh spew of hot water.

Perhaps it was listening to my grandmas' stories of the Great Depression that instilled in me a scarcity mindset that I could lose everything at any moment. Or it could've been the deep respect I had for my parents who worked so hard to guarantee that us kids had just enough. I would hate to make a decision where I could lose money after all my parents did for us. Maybe it came from growing up with the motto that we should save because we don't know what might happen. I never thought I could save enough for any situation that could arise.

Or it could be that the fear of not being able to take care of myself came from living most of my life alone. I had this feeling deep inside that the rest of my life I would be living my life on my own. There was a fear of loneliness there that threatened my confidence and made me think that being unable to take care of myself would be my worst nightmare[1].

---

1. In recent years, this isn't as much of a fear as I've learned about how amazing assisted living facilities can be. There are places that come with state-of-the-art fitness centers, swimming pools, pickleball courts, and an ambitious social calendar of events. I've been researching these for my mom, and they sound fabulous!

Whatever the reason, it was clear that after losing my job and receiving the Big Kahuna, I was facing my biggest fear.

It was head-spinning just how fast my life had changed from walking into my house and my spine giving out to losing a job that had given me more than just a paycheck—it gave me purpose. My ego and identity were Pat the Athlete and Pat the Diamond Lady. *Who am I now, if not these things?*

My future looked completely unfamiliar to me as my spinal fusion recovery was set for two years. *Does that mean I'll be unable to work that whole time? How am I going to pay my bills? How much more will I have to give up?*

On top of my potential financial downfall, my physical fear of needing help was even scarier. It's hard to worry about work when you can't put your shoes on, or when you drop something and you can't pick it up. There were times I couldn't go to the bathroom and wipe myself. And days upon days when I couldn't get out of bed.

I had never been so tested and took for granted how lucky I'd been before my injury to see many more good days than bad ones in my life. I was grieving the woman I had always expected to be–the fit lady still swinging a tennis racket until I was ninety, yup ninety. At the time, I wasn't sure I'd ever live pain-free or be able to even walk around my block.

My first instinct in facing this upheaval of my life was to want to fly away and ignore what the Universe was throwing at me. After a few days of this mindset though, I realized it wasn't serving me. To cultivate the resiliency and strength needed to move on from this trauma, I needed to battle back against the depression, isolation, fear, and hopelessness I was experiencing. I was on a mission to figure out who I was now and how I was going to push through.

I take comfort in the power and resourcefulness of eagles. I started this chapter with wisdom from Jack White about eagles and how they use storms that come their way to lift them higher above the rain. When a storm hits, an eagle sets its wings to use the wind's power to soar above the storm. Often, in those first few weeks of recovery while I was sitting in bed at my mom's, unable to get up, I would picture myself as an eagle soaring above the storm of my life.

During this time, I came across another quote about eagles by Abdul Kalam, which states, "*All birds find shelter during a rain. But eagles avoid rain by flying above the clouds. Problems are common, but attitude makes the difference.*" While eagles use *altitude* to get in and out of storms, it's our *attitude* that makes the difference when facing our greatest fears. When we face dark clouds and rise above them, our outlook on life changes. The storm is coming whether we want it to or not, and sometimes all you can control is your attitude. One's viewpoint is the most important tool available and learning to leverage personal storms to your advantage takes a special set of muscles. To overcome, you may have to leave things that are weighing you down. Old patterns, relationships, and beliefs may no longer serve you, and that's okay. It takes different stamina to fight when life is throwing you curveball after curveball.

For me, the first step to recalibrating my life and facing my fears head-on was accepting that I'd never be the same. I would never look the same or be as strong as I was. This was especially true for my left leg that looked like a half-filled water balloon. My nerves weren't talking to my muscles, so the muscles just hung there. My skin looked old and wrinkled, and my leg sagged. I had been a life-long triathlete, tennis player, and sailor—I didn't have legs or muscles that sagged. Plus, my dad had great strong legs his entire life, and *lucky me* got his genes.

I focused on sitting with myself, trying to listen to my body even if I hated the messages: I'll never play tennis again, go for a trail run, or jump onto the wave runner. I had to accept that my life was now separated into two worlds: the world before my leg exploded walking into my house, and this new, uncharted world of injury and recovery. I will never be that previous Pat again, which is often heartbreaking because I really liked that Pat.

Old-world Pat was an adult who never really had to grow up. I had my health, a fulfilling job, and no life-long partner or children. I was free to give my time, energy, and support to others. I volunteered for the Red Cross and loved being the Lake Travis Thunder Special Olympics swim team coach. I was happy-go-lucky, and that's what attracted people to me (or so I thought).

The world feels bigger when you are the giver—the one that takes care of everyone and is always there to help. When my greatest fear came knocking at my door, my world felt suddenly smaller. Now, I was the one with needs, with fewer possibilities of what I could do on my own or for others, and that change was wildly uncomfortable. The discomfort was whispering to me, telling me I had to learn how to say no to commitments that I once loved and ask for help despite it being foreign to me.

I had to stop envisioning what I thought was my future—marathons, reaching down to scoop up a tennis ball, and sitting in a car for hours on a road trip. Driving was something I loved doing, but since I couldn't sit longer than an hour, I would have to make different choices. I was impatient, but I would need time to adjust to my new reality and visualize how I would fit in and function in my new world.

I was realizing that this back injury was going to change my life *permanently*. The strong, can-do-anything type that my friends and family saw was no longer me. As soon as that thought hit me though, I became defensive. *I don't want to be different. I don't want to change.* Focusing on those statements became wasted energy, me just trying to swim against the tide. They tempted me to obsess about my past, scrolling through old pictures of me on adventures, and believing that the best years of my life were behind me. Mustering courage to fight against that belief, I forced myself to slow down and be present with myself, facing the hard facts so that I could move on and recover. Your mind can take you on any number of paths, but learning to control it begins with being honest about your circumstances. With acceptance of your situation, you tend to see the truth of who you are now—whether the scars are physical or emotional—and that allows you to usher in the ability to create your next game plan.

During the months leading up to the Big Kahuna, I had an amazing therapist, Pam. I kept bringing up to her how terrified I was of the three and a half hour drive it would take to get from Rochester, Minnesota to my mom's place in Iowa where I would recover after the surgery. Every time I thought about this logistic, I would feel anxiety pour over me, believing that it would be almost too painful of an experience for me to go through. The idea of surgery was scary but being in a car for that long post-surgery felt like a freaking nightmare.

Pam was an angel and helped me week after week leading up to the surgery. She led me through visualization exercises that she wanted me to implore when the time came for me to be on that drive. I was to picture my happy place, which was my beautiful dock on Lake Travis on the most perfect of Austin days. I pictured myself looking out on the lake seeing the sunshine so brilliantly on the water that I'd be reminded of sparkling diamonds. I could see a bird land on the lake, creating calm ripples of water that mesmerized me. I imagined the feeling of diving into that lake on a hot day and the instant refreshment that would wash over me. It would feel so incredible that I would laugh out loud from the pure joy of it all. I visualized myself swimming, listening to the sound of my arms gracefully coming in and out of the water as I did my swim strokes. This was my happy place, my safe place, my calm place, my place of peace where fear had no invitation.

I repeated these images in my head over and over again when the time came for that drive, and miraculously, the anxiety I had been building up for months did not win out. Thanks to Pam, I was able to change that narrative and get through it by holding onto the good in my life.

On the other side of fear is reimagining. Fear after all is only a figment of one's imagination. If I could imagine a future I was afraid of, I also had the capacity to imagine a different future, one where I would be okay, one where I could thrive. I would need to do this to not be terrified of my new life. First though, I had to change the narrative around my identity. I realized that the qualities I had measured my identity by before—athletic prowess and success in my job—

were not good enough as they proved able to be taken away from me. Thus, I had to come up with a new definition for identity. What truly comprises your identity are characteristics that if you had *nothing* or *everything* wouldn't change. As I sat with this idea, I realized that if old-world Pat had been asked if she could handle what was about to happen to her, she would've doubted if she could. She couldn't have summoned in her mind a situation that took away almost everything about her lifestyle and purpose. She would've been overwhelmed by it.

Here I was though, still living, leaning into this new life, and that's when it hit me: at my core I am a *fighter*. Even with my circumstances turned completely upside down, I was still a fighter. I was still the one pushing the limits even if those limits felt smaller than before. Nothing, not even *fear*, could take that away from me.

Once again, I was reminded of eagles. Eagles weather the storm because they need to fly. They can't sit and survive on their own without flying. Even in the midst of chaos, they rise above. That's what I would do. I would channel the courage of an eagle who has no choice but to fly. I was going to fly.

Hope Nugget: A fighter attitude doesn't change your circumstances, but it can give you wings you didn't know you had.

Chapter 5

The Greatest Hero

"I want to die. I want to be done!"

More than once, this would be my admission to my own mother, the woman who birthed me, who now, at nearly ninety years of age, was taking care of my every need as I maneuvered the horrors of recovery. I would be living with her for at least seven months in Des Moines, Iowa—the place of my childhood and coming of age. Something about this journey of recovery felt like another coming of age. Thankfully, I once again had the amazing care of my mom even if my ego was struggling with my dependence on her.

The youngest of three, my mom was a born and bred Midwesterner who grew up in a pretty strict household in Hinsdale, Illinois, a suburb on the outskirts of Chicago. She was an incredible figure skater who made sure her offspring learned to skate before we could even walk. She went to all Catholic schools and lived in a home that overlooked St.

Isaac Jogues Parish[1]. It's a gorgeous church, and my grandfather cleaned it. My mom was baptized, married, and then became a teacher, all at that church.

I mentioned before that my mom would say she had a sister who was a nun, a brother who was a priest, and that she married a saint. This is because her oldest sister, my Aunt Michele, became a Catholic nun. Her brother became a Catholic priest and a missionary to the Philippines and Taiwan. Sadly, at the age of thirty-five, Father Bernard Doyle got a form of Hodgkin's disease and died. It was terrible. He was a brilliant man who gave his life to beautiful, generous pursuits for the benefit of others. He helped build a private Catholic university in Tai Pei, Taiwan called "Fu Jen University". The university was founded in 1925 in Beijing at the request of Pope Pius XI and re-established in Taiwan in 1961 at the request of Pope John XXIII. Its name means "assistance" and "benevolence". I was blessed to be able to visit the university once when I was in Taiwan for work. It was so special to be able to walk the halls and see past photos of my uncle, the same photos my parents and grandparents had of him at home.

The saint, of course, was my dad. She never fell out of love with him, and humor was their love language. She loved teasing him and they played jokes on each other all the time. I'll never forget the accidental joke he played on her though.

My mom, dad, and I were on vacation visiting my sister Carol who lived in Switzerland at the time. We were all at some mountain overlooking this gorgeous scenic view. My mother put a lot of hairspray in her hair and the bees there

---

1. Whenever I stayed with my grandparents, I would peek out the window of the room I was staying in, hoping I would see a nun's shadow pass by.

were loving her hair. My dad's bad habit had always been to chew on toothpicks. He would chew on toothpicks and then toss them, and we would find toothpicks all over the place. My mother hated it.

While taking in the scenic Swiss view, bees were driving mom crazy and since she's allergic she screamed and ran in the car to get away from them. As she jumped in the car, she felt two bees sting her butt. She screamed even louder, alerting me to rush and make sure she was' okay. As I got to the car, she turned her butt to me and yelled, "Get them off of me! *Get them off!*" I looked at her rear end, took a brief sigh in relief, and then started cracking up. Bees hadn't stung her; she had simply sat on toothpicks my dad had left in the seats of the van. I (graciously) picked them out of her butt, but I can't ever remember a time that we all laughed harder than that moment.

My mom became a very proud flight attendant for American Airlines. In those days you had to be unmarried, have the perfect weight and shape, and come with flawless nails to become a flight attendant. Mom has always been gorgeous, always looking like she has walked off the cover of a magazine. She was on the first flight out of Chicago Midway airport on American Airlines, and one of her craziest stories is that she accidentally spilled breakfast on Nat King Cole. Oops! To this day, she's still so proud of being an AA flight attendant and keeps her old uniforms (a different one for each season) in pristine condition.

I always thought it so ironic that here I am a gritty, mountain biking, triathlon participant, open water swimmer, and so forth with a mom who would give Jackie Kennedy a run for her money. That is how we are opposites, but in other ways we are very similar.

Positivity and humor were some of those similarities (she had the nickname Betty White), but now the once positive Pat was struggling to navigate the misery of pain being synonymous with breathing. Often in those moments, I was genuine in my desire to give up everything if it meant no longer living like this. The voice in my head could twirl me in circles of seeing only the burden I was to the people I loved. In the thick of what felt like an endless recovery, I dove straight into a mental black hole, one where no light could be seen. Well, except for one—my guardian angel, a holy being, an Irish lass who embodied faith more than any human I'd come across—my mom. Black holes are no match for angels.

She always knew what to say and her words were filled with grace. When I imagine the influence Jesus can have on a person, I picture my mother as the epitome of that. This has influenced me tremendously. Whenever I'm in a hard season, it is faith that keeps me going. I choose to believe, and I still go to church. And in the moments when I become frustrated with the world, God, or my religion, I remember my mom's words and I pray to Mary.

Though I knew her heart hurt to see me overwhelmed by sadness, she didn't let that dictate her own mentality. Instead, she used her gifts to elevate the atoms bouncing around whatever room she was in until hope could be picked out and seen by all around her. Thankfully, I was not immune to her skills.

When I spoke of these desperate thoughts, my mom didn't hush me or tell me I was being dramatic or that my feelings weren't valid. She didn't express that my words were hurting her (though on occasion I saw little, silent tears roll down her cheeks). She didn't sugarcoat my pain and give me her opinions on the purpose of my suffering. What she did was listen. She took my hand and just listened.

Then she went into action. Her mission became to be my caregiver, and I cannot imagine a more loving, compassionate, wise, and funny caregiver than her. She wiped my butt when I couldn't, she cleaned my incisions, and she, more often than I care to admit, talked me off a cliff by making me laugh.

Unfortunately, it didn't take long for me to begin worrying about the toll caregiving was taking on my mom. Though she wasn't showing me any signs of weakness, I knew the empath in her was taking on my feelings and pain. Even though she always showed up with a smile, I knew this must be devastating for her.

One day I talked to my mom's best friend, Mary Jane, letting her know of my concerns for my mom and how much pressure my situation was putting on her life. Her friend didn't hesitate for a moment before responding, "She loves it, Pat. She wants this. She wouldn't want it any other way. She feels purpose in caring for you."

Unconvinced, I went to mom myself and voiced my worries about the impact I was having on her. She listened and then stated confidently, "Pat, do not worry about me. I think God has kept me so healthy and independent because I am needed. We all desire to be needed, and you needing me is keeping me alive. Just let me care for you, my girl."

Care for me she did, tending to not only my physical needs, but my emotional ones as well. If I wasn't out of my bedroom by late morning, she would come in and make sure I got dressed for the day. Some days she'd find me lying in bed bawling and when she came in, I would ask, "Why would God do this to me? Why? I don't understand why this is happening to me!"

"I don't know why either, Pat. All I know is that you're going to get through it," she lovingly replied. Then she would give me a hug and say something like, "Why don't you come out and eat something?"

Over our three meals together each day (even if at least one of those was just some peanut butter and crackers), Mom managed to dish me up a plate of laughter. My mom has humor as a core value, knowing it is one of the best medicines the world has to offer, and if anything, that is her legacy to me. Laughing made me feel better, and though there were numerous times I struggled to laugh with my mom, somehow in her strong, faithful way she managed to get a smile out of me even on the worst days of my life.

In the mornings, we loved to watch *Good Morning America* as we adored Lara Spencer and Robin Roberts and their entertaining segments that would spark silly or sometimes serious conversations among us. Mom loved to comment on the fashion choices of the female anchors, often saying something like, "Oh, I love Robin's dress! You'd look great in that, Pat." Her colorful commentary no matter what we watched was a life saver. If no other positive thing existed in my day, at least I had these moments to soak up and smile about. Those moments were, and still are, everything.

I was having one of my worst days, feeling lost and completely pushed over the edge. I was lying on top of my bed in my clothes uncontrollably crying. I knew Mom was in the back room, and that she knew I was upset, but she let me cry for a while. Eventually she came in and asked how I was doing to which I only replied with more crying. She hugged me for a few minutes, and when she eventually pulled away, looked me straight in the eye with all the compassion and empathy in the world. I could tell she was about to say something wise, so I stared back into her piercing blue eyes.

"David Muir is on in ten minutes," she said with a smile. Then she got up and left the room, hoping I would snag the bait.

It wasn't exactly the wisdom I expected to hear, but that's because her Jedi mind tricks are far superior to mine. Watching ABC's *World News Tonight* was a ritual for my mom, and one I adopted as I lived with her. Her big crush on the lead anchor David Muir always meant I would be entertained by mom's comments on David's eloquent speech, perfectly combed over hair, and smoldering smile, which made me burst out laughing every time. It was our thing and she wanted to make sure I didn't miss it. After we finished watching and were headed to bed, she smiled and said, "Remember Pat, tomorrow is a holiday, so sleep in." It wasn't any official holiday, but this was her way of taking pressure off of me.

There was another day after my surgery that my body was super messed up and my hormones were all over the place. I had just had it and for some reason my body decided that it was going to have a period. I'd had premature menopause, so I hadn't had a period since I was forty and so here I was fifty-six and I am suddenly bleeding all over the place. My first thought was, "Oh shit, I must be bleeding internally." Who knows what happens when they put rods and screws in you?

I have a very good friend, Dr. Renee Lockey, who is a

brilliant OB-GYN and surgeon. I called her immediately to ask her if this was internal bleeding.

"No, Pat. These things can happen when your body goes through something extreme and is all messed up. It's a period."

As she tells me it's all going to be okay, I am standing in the hallway with the woman who helped me navigate puberty as a preteen while I am holding bloody undies and stained sweats (of course I was wearing white sweatpants that day). I hang up the phone and Mom and I look at each other for a beat before she bursts out laughing. I was crying, but now I started laughing too. For fuck's sake! On top of everything, I had to get a period too. It was so absurd we just had to lose it and allow laughter to vibrate along the hallway.

There is no one I'd rather have as the captain of my team than my mom. Unwaveringly strong, she became my rock, my person, my advocate, and the one who I have in my mind as I push myself to heal and grow stronger. She deserves to see me win in my recovery. When I need to dig deep for motivation, I close my eyes and imagine a day I can boldly declare myself pain-free. Then I picture my mom taking me to Wendy's for a Frosty celebration just like she did after my childhood swim meets. Some things just stick with you.

"I wish you enough" is an old Irish saying that I grew up with. My Grandmother Doyle would say this, and mom took it on as well. Mom would sign all her letters with that phrase in hopes that all would have enough love, money, health, and happiness to sustain them. The Irish blessing goes:

May you have . . .
enough happiness to keep you sweet,
enough trials to keep you strong,

enough sorrow to keep you human,
enough hope to keep you happy,
enough failure to keep you humble,
enough success to keep you eager,
enough wealth to meet your needs,
enough enthusiasm to look forward,
enough friends to give you comfort,
enough faith to banish depression,
enough determination to make each day
better than yesterday.

As I became an adult, I never thought I was enough. I always wanted to be better. After surviving the fire of all my physical and emotional challenges though, I was beginning to think that maybe I was enough. Maybe I could stop trying to prove that it was so and just believe that truth. No matter how broken I was in body and spirit, I still had value and a life of meaning. I was *enough*, scars and all, and in the moments I forgot, Mom would glide in with the utmost grace, and remind me.

Hope Nugget: If you don't have one, find a great maternal role model. Our greatest heroes are the mothers of the world.

Chapter 6

Even Titanium Breaks

For the past six years, a group of friends and I have made a commitment to take a hiking trip to a national park once a year. We've hiked trails in Yellowstone, Rocky Mountain, and Glacier national parks. I loved our group of hikers as the comradery established on these trips was always affirming and elevating. Though I appreciated the personal elevation, I hated the physical part of these trips. I am terrified of heights, and on our nature hikes the group always pushed me to go farther than I did the previous year. Thus, these trips tested my mental strength as much as my physical prowess. It felt good to face my fears, even if I had to turn around before making the peak, even if I was bitching, crying, and complaining the whole hike. Ultimately, I was grateful to be pushed out of my comfort zone. Doing something I couldn't believe I would do was thrilling.

Nine months after my Big Kahuna surgery, the group traveled to Tennessee to hike the Great Smoky Mountains. Never one to say no to an adventure, I joined my friends. Though I thought I'd face numerous mental and physical hurdles before, this trip felt like a marathon paired with the steeplechase. As we ventured away from our basecamp and up the mountains, I watched as my group thundered ahead of me. Though my friend Joanna offered to stay behind with me, I declined. I didn't want to hinder others' personal goals. "I'll be fine," I uttered adamantly, plastering a fake smile on my face. I felt so responsible for battling this on my own and not inhibiting someone else's experience.

It only took a few minutes for the entire group to be out of my sight. As I watched the last of my team turn a corner out of my vision, I let my shoulders sag, and tears began to form in my eyes. My ego felt like it had just been stabbed with a thousand needles. I let the battle between my heart and my reality have some space. *This isn't me. This isn't me.* But then I approached a narrow section of stairs I had to hike up. Stairs were extremely difficult for my left leg, which I could barely feel and had lost its muscle mass. I couldn't put full weight on it so as I went up the stairs, I had to use my arms to pull my left leg up each step, one by one. This took all of my focus and, in that moment, I could not deny that this person struggling to go up what many would think was the easiest part of the hike, was in fact me. This was me right now. Maybe not forever, but for now. I was the crippled hiker, the one that couldn't keep up.

I paused for a moment, closed my eyes, and took a deep breath searching my mind for a positive voice. Words my mom said to me right before I headed out for this trip hit my memory, "You're such an encouragement and inspiration to us, Pat." I could hear the exact lilt of her voice as she said that to me, and I began re-playing her words until it felt like she was right beside me cheering me on. My mom is the strongest woman I know, full of integrity, and if she said those words, I knew she meant them.

I opened my eyes and continued my sloth-like trek up the peak with a slew of new mantras running through my mind and, at times, boldly coming out of mouth[1]:

Pat, you're an inspiration.

Pat, you can do hard things.

Pat, you are climbing a mountain after two back surgeries.

Pat, there's nothing you can't do.

Despite the mantras or maybe because of them, the tears escaped my eyes and began rolling down my cheeks. I was grateful for my sunglasses, but wished I had giant ones like movie stars wear. Mine weren't cutting it as a wall to hide behind. I kept aggressively wiping the tears away, not wanting to flood the ground with my emotions.

As I continued my ascent, I began coming to terms with my mom's words. If I was truly to be an inspiration, I couldn't hide my struggle. I had to own it. I wasn't here to blend in, and though I wished my struggle wasn't so visible, this was my reality. Now it was up to me to decide what to do with it. With that thought, I switched gears, not caring if people saw my struggle. My ego cringed with that choice, but I was celebrating the fact that I wasn't allowing my ego to rule my life. Humility would have to replace her.

I'm sure I was a sight to see as after this revelation, I was practically crawling up the mountain on all fours, grabbing my leg, and struggling with my trekking poles I'd pulled out. Slowly, minute by minute, second by second, progress was

---

1. Of course, I also uttered other less inspiring phrases such as "This sucks!" Or "Aggghh fuck this!"

being made. With labored breath and aching muscles, sweat formed in every crevice of my body. My brain could no longer think about what people were thinking around me. All it could fathom was focusing on the next step before me, and the next one and the next one and the next one until, by some miracle, I made it to the turnaround point to begin my descent. *Hallelujah! Halle-Freaking-Lujah!!!!* I made it up the mountain! I reached my goal! *I can do hard things!*

But, damn, I needed a break.

There was nowhere to sit so I rested by plopping my butt down right on the trail. It was excruciatingly embarrassing as other climbers had to literally step over me to keep on their hike, but I was in survival mode. I grabbed a PB&J sandwich from my backpack, and with no shame started munching away. As I did, a group of hikers walked by asking me how I was doing, and if I needed anything. "No thanks, I'm good. Really good."

Another group came by with huge smiles on their faces. "We've been watching you and you're doing amazing! Congrats on making it this far."

I didn't want to accept their praise, but I fought against my discomfort and allowed myself to believe that I was accomplishing something noteworthy. I smiled back at their words with a hearty "Thank you," and repeated them in my head until I came to grips with their sincerity.

After thirty minutes, I stood up, ready to continue my trek back down the mountain. But first I took in my surroundings. Gratitude overwhelmed me as I realized the majesty all around. I was overlooking a bright green valley with thousands of trees. Being autumn, some trees had begun to change colors and the different hues I was experiencing in one view made my breath catch. The view seemed endless as if the beauty all around me would never end. Sunlight glistened amongst the mountain, and the glow reminded me of the sparkle that ignites in a natural diamond when the light hits it just right. Oh, how inspired the human race is by nature. We are constantly working on ways to replicate it, but it never once measures up to it. You just can't capture divine creation. It is far too miraculous. I was happy not to be missing this moment. It was a struggle for both my body and soul, but I was here. I showed up, and this view was my reward. For the first time in my life, I didn't care that I came in last.

After over six hours of hiking, I arrived back at the base-camp where it was all smiles and thumbs up from fellow hikers for completing what I did. Only ten minutes later, my crew reached basecamp too.

"How'd it go, Pat?"

"I went farther than I thought I could go. Made it up to where it started to get steep and then sat in the middle of the trail and ate lunch. Then came back down."

"That's amazing! You must've hiked at least six miles."

"Pat, you're such a badass!"

"I'm so proud of you!"

They were shocked I hiked that long and reached the height I did. Though I thought it was pitiful in comparison to what I used to do, I accepted their undeniable excitement for me. I didn't share the emotional upheaval I went through and the glorious insights I gained. It just didn't feel right at that moment. Now was a time to celebrate the physical feat. Maybe I'd share those revelations with them when they weren't so fresh.

Their encouragement lifted me up and felt like physical proof that I could do anything I set my mind to. I was flying high, and in that moment, hope flew into my heart like a long-lost friend returning to me.

Unfortunately, that feeling didn't last long. As I headed to bed that night, something was wrong. For the first time since my surgery, I was hearing a scraping sound in my right ear. I had no idea what it was, but it made me think my bones or rods were rubbing against each other, which was not a pleasant visual. I told myself it was probably nothing, and that I should ignore it and get some rest, but I only believed that half-heartedly.

Two weeks after my six-hour hike, I was back in the yoga studio. I walked in and threw my jacket in the personal items bin by the front door when I heard a crack so deafening that my friend Gwyn hollered from across the room, "What was that?""

"My back," I squeaked.

I decided to ignore the noise and stay in my yoga class. I could deal with whatever was going on afterward. As I started the class, I could tell something in my back was off. Moving felt weird, and I was afraid of irritating anything further, so I spent most of the class in resting poses.

Toward the end of the class, the teacher was helping each of us get into what is known as "crow pose." I was always trying to get this pose down, but never quite could because your back simply isn't that flexible when your lower lumbar is fused. I didn't want to give up an opportunity to practice though. Shaking all thoughts of my back, I focused solely on the pose. I slowly planted both hands on the floor, rested my shins upon my upper arms, and used my upper body strength to lift my feet up. I was shaking, but soon realized my butt and legs were in the air. I was doing the crow! Today, of all days, I was able to get in the pose. Ha!

Gwyn saw me and got excited. "Pat, you're doing it!" Then she grabbed her phone and took a picture of me checking off the balance pose I'd always wanted to be able to do. I smiled at her, but once I un-posed myself, I was hurting. Thankfully, the class was ending.

I didn't stay to chat with anyone, but immediately limped out of class and headed straight toward my local doctor. Now that I didn't have yoga to distract me, my entire body was shaking with anxiety. What just happened to me?

The doctor took me back to get an X-ray straight away, and within twenty minutes of receiving the results, my Mayo surgeon's team called me.

"Pat, you have to come back here for surgery. All your rods and screws have broken."

What? For fuck's sake! My mind went into overdrive, and I began to panic. My rods and screws broke? How in the world did I break my back again? I couldn't grasp what was happening. No one had warned me that my *titanium* rods and screws could break.

"I am fucked. Seriously fucked." This was the phrase put on repeat as I shakily drove myself back home.

Once I was back in my house, I could no longer ignore the sound of my bones and rods scraping against each other. The melody alone was terrifying, far worse than nails on a chalkboard. I was afraid to breathe. If I took a whiff of air through my mouth, I could feel a rod moving, popping, and shifting. If I blinked, it seemed like my spine shifted. I held my head as straight as I could and didn't want to reach for my phone or remote because though it wasn't super painful, when I moved it felt like my spine was flowing back and forth like an earthquake.

Shock and disbelief overwhelmed every molecule in me until uncontrollable tears burst forth. I tried to control my breathing. I couldn't afford the movement that would happen if a full-on physical breakdown took place.

My doctors had told me that my progress after the first surgery was in the top one percent, and still, this happened. I did everything I was told to do. Though the rebel in me frequently breaks rules, this time I followed all of my doctors' orders. I was ten months into my two-year recovery, and the worst truth was becoming apparent. I would need to hit the restart button all over again.

I knew I couldn't keep this news to myself, but I was afraid to tell my mom. After all the support, caretaking, and comfort she'd given me the first time, I didn't want to break her heart with this news and burden her again. I called my sister Joanne but could barely talk or even breathe. I somehow sputtered out, "Everything broke. It broke. I have to get another fusion."

Just saying those words aloud brought on an onslaught of choking tears. *Damn it.* Joanne soothed me with words of kindness and the truth that I was not going into this alone. This led me to call a few close friends with the news who echoed the same message. No matter what, I didn't have to face this alone. I knew I had to call Mom next. She needed to hear it from me. Luckily, my sister Carol happened to be with my mom, so she didn't have to hear my upsetting news alone. My voice was shaking as I told her about the next feat I was up against. I cringed as I waited for her response, worried I had disappointed her and feeling guilty that I'd need her help again to recover after my second Big Kahuna surgery—something we had never even considered as a possibility.

Ever the cool cucumber, my mom didn't hesitate for a moment. "Honey, it's okay. We'll get through this together. You've done it before, and you can do it again." Silent, hopeful tears streamed down my face as her words acted as a soothing well to my fiery, troubled heart. Yes, *we* could do it again.

Getting Back on the Train

My train had derailed. I had to go back to the beginning of this journey once more. My initial reactions were, "Hell, no, I don't want to get on that train again." Who could I trust? I didn't want to trust anybody. I had tried to do everything right. I tried to be "that person" who shows up and rebuilds and fuses back into life. But I didn't want to anymore.

Not only that, a second surgery would be more complicated as they had to take my titanium equipment out and replace it with cobalt rods and screws. This meant my recovery would start all over again. Regaining mobility and getting some semblance of my active lifestyle back would be slower after the second surgery.

The irony was not lost to me that I had been a professional in the jewelry industry for thirty-five years and was extremely familiar with titanium and cobalt. Titanium is one of the world's toughest metals. It ranks high in strength but is lightweight. My replacement screws and rods would be made from cobalt, another of the world's strongest metals. The sturdiest airplanes and boats are made out of cobalt.

Cobalt is not as malleable as titanium and has less chance to fracture. Would cobalt work? I had to take a leap of faith and see, but it was heartbreaking to be halfway to the finish line and be moved back to the starting block.

GET OFF THE BLAME BANDWAGON

I felt like a failure. I must have done something wrong. My doctors at Mayo assured me there was nothing I could've done. "These things happen," they told me. I wanted an answer, but they didn't have answers. No one could tell me why this was happening, and I was frustrated. My friends and neighbors were in an uproar looking to blame someone with ideas of suing my doctors or the company that made my titanium equipment. Everybody wanted answers as if an explanation would somehow protect them from my fate. The general feeling I got was, "She must have done too much. She pushed herself too far. It's Pat's fault."

I got to a point where I didn't want to talk about it. I was obsessively replaying everything over and over again trying to search for a logical answer. Did my body just not fuse in time? Every body is different, and everyone's surgeries are different. For some reason, this is the path I have to walk. I don't know why. *Aggghhhhh!* Finally, in order to quiet my mind, I came to the conclusion that I'm just a badass who can break titanium.

It had been ten months since my first fusion surgery and eighteen months since I'd walked into my home and fallen down. I had waited so long to have my first surgery at Mayo and hated that I was going backward. After surgery, it had been work, work, work, show up, build a resiliency mindset, and *repeat*. A new surgery would mean an additional two-year recovery.

My life of showing up came to an abrupt end. All the doubts and questions I had worked so hard to move past were at the front of my mind again. All my hopes and positivity were destroyed. I was giving in to despair when this loud, demanding voice deep within me asked, "What are your options?"

I was stumped. What options did I have? Jump off a bridge? Land in a wheelchair for the rest of my life? Ugh, were there any good options left?

"Okay, Pat, ultimately you can choose to give up, give in, or get it done." I was in the habit of speaking to myself out loud when faced with huge decisions.

As I heard these words out loud, a stillness came over me, and I knew my only option was to get it done and do this whole thing all over again. If I wanted a chance to live some semblance of an active life, I had to show up and be tested as I had never been before.

I couldn't comprehend how I would move forward, but I took it one painstakingly cruel step at a time. I had just started building a business with some jewelry industry colleagues, and now I would have to close that part of my life and give away my earnings to other people who could complete the work that was promised. Once again, I would be alone with no work and walking away from the new community I had built at the fitness club. I was leaving my girlfriends and neighbors, physical therapist, yoga teachers, and spin-class friends—all for the hope that I'd be back active again someday. I would not only have to rebuild and refuse my spine again, but I would have to rebuild a community too. My ego was taking another hard kick in the ass as I mourned the loss of my recovery and prepared to go to my mom's house in Iowa once more.

It Might Not Be Your Lesson

As I began letting friends know what had happened, people cried, and asked me, "How did this happen, to you of all people?" No one could believe I had to start over and relive the last ten months. *I* still couldn't believe it. As I made plans for a second Mayo surgery, I questioned how I'd find the fire again. How do I get the fight? Why does God do this to someone who gives back, is a good person, who needs her strength to give back to her community and return to coaching her Special Olympics swim team? In my head and my prayers, I kept asking *why me?* After a few days of panicking and confusion, and a few more days where God was silent, I came to an answer: *Why not me?*

This realization was mostly inspired by my aunt, Sister Michele Doyle, who has been a nun of the School Sisters of St. Francis for seventy-six years. My aunt spent more than five decades in Mississippi as a Catholic school teacher, college professor, and parish religious education leader. She's one of the wisest people I know, and in my struggle to come to terms with this fate, I asked her why God would put me through this again. Her answer was simple and straightforward, "God didn't do this to you. Your back did this to you." *Whoa.* She continued, "It's not that you didn't learn what God wanted you to the first time. What's happening to you now might not be your lesson."

It was so powerful to believe that I wasn't being punished and understood that what I was going through might be an example, encouragement, or a message someone else needed. Perhaps I was being used as the conduit to someone else's journey or enlightenment. I was so short sighted in my thinking that this was all about me.

The minute she said that, I thought, *I'm going to look for that person who needs this lesson and give them a piece of my mind.* But first I was going to rest in the peace Aunt Michele's words gave me. I didn't do anything wrong, my surgeons didn't do anything wrong, and my body didn't purposely wrong me. This might not be my lesson, but I would fight through it like the underdog I was.

When You Need a Wall to Lean On

I had been attending a regular yoga class before the break and would always go to the same corner wall of the studio because I needed support to do certain poses and stretches. Everybody knew that was *my corner*, like in church, where your family sits in the same spot Sunday after Sunday. No one really knew what I was going through, but they understood I needed that spot, and they'd tell people to move if someone unknowingly laid their mat there. There was this cool-looking guy with a gentle soul, Carlos, who always protected my spot. He didn't know my situation, but he understood I needed those walls.

When my yoga instructor told the class that I'd had a second break, the class decided that was still my spot, and it would be waiting for me when I recovered. We all need walls to lean on and people who will save our spots. When she told me this, I was reminded that there are many people on your team that you don't even know are rooting for you. And even as alone as you might feel, there's a community out there to find.

There was another person I desperately needed to tell about this second fusion, and I was dreading it nearly as much as telling my mom—Monica Sherman-Peter.

I met Monica at Benedictine College. Benedictine was a small, Catholic college where you knew everyone. Five Henneberrys had attended Benedictine College, and I loved keeping that record alive. Monica was a couple of years older than me, and I remember always looking up to her. She was a great athlete who played on the tennis team with my sister Joanne, always seemed effortlessly cool, and she had a super nice boyfriend named Greg (who she eventually married). Anytime I got to spend time with her and her upperclassmen friends was a blast, and made me feel cool and like I was on top of the world.

We lost touch after college. We had been in different grades, and went our separate ways, until one day thirty-seven years after college, and five months after my fusion, I received a message from her. She'd been going through hell of her own. Numerous difficulties including having tragically lost three of her five children over the years. Now she'd hurt her back and was being advised that she needed a spinal fusion of her own. She was the epitome of resiliency. In her research, she had stumbled upon a recent article Mayo wrote about me and my fusion, which had led to her call.

"Is that you in that Mayo article, Pat?" she asked.

"Yes, it is."

Thus, began a divine friendship I couldn't be more grateful for. We started talking almost daily after that, and I finally felt like I could give back with my experiences from my back surgery. We talked about everything—recovery, back surgery in detail, insurance hell, what happened to me, what happened to her. We would send each other text messages with links to research we found on our surgeries or various physical therapy exercises we wanted to try. We would cry with understanding for what the other was going through and commiserate over how the waiting period is always the worst. We had so much in common with our Midwestern roots (she was from Nebraska) and our love for athletics, and with each passing week, our connection closed the distance of not having talked for so long. It felt like it'd only been a year since we last talked, rather than thirty. She was my Benedictine sister.

She decided to go forth with a fusion, which was slated for November 20th. When I was told that my rods had broken and I would need another fusion, Monica immediately flashed through my mind. I was supposed to be the one who had been through this and could encourage her. I'd been so excited to coach and inspire on the other side of this surgery. Now, I was going to have to be the bearer of the most discouraging news I could think of. *What am I going to tell her as she prepares for a fusion, and mine just failed? Would she believe me now that there was a light at the end of her struggle?*

To make matters crazier, my second fusion was scheduled for the day before her first one. Her fusion had been scheduled for November 20th, and Mayo would be doing mine November 19th. It was so difficult making that call. I almost considered not even telling her, but I knew that we were too connected now for it not to come up in the future. She deserved to know, so with my stomach in knots, I picked up that phone and dialed her number.

As always, Monica's reaction was a gift. She handled it so graciously, directing so much of her attention on how I was handling the news. I assured her this was so rare, and there was almost no chance it would happen to her. She encouraged me and listened and never made me feel bad for telling her. We laughed at the fact that we would both be in recovery at the same time and took comfort in knowing we would be there for one another, us Benedictine sisters, ready to lift each other up through this crazy journey. It's amazing how God puts the right people in your life at the right time. It makes you believe you can handle anything.

Though my perspective had shifted, it wasn't long before fear, discouragement, and weakness showed their ugly heads. I was exhausted and starting over felt insurmountable. I knew I needed to dig deep, practicing all the lessons I had learned the first go around, but all I wanted to do was curl in a ball and give up.

Thus, the return of my frantic search for hope.

Thankfully, I had a whole team behind me. The night before I was set to head back to Mayo and begin the preliminary evaluations for my second fusion, some amazing friends came over to my house to hang out with me. They brought over dinner and did their best to keep me calm before my flight the next morning. As we were chatting about my fears and worries over another surgery, my friend Anne had an idea.

"Pat, I bet there's a saint for backs!"

"There's not going to be a saint for back pain," I replied. I was in a foul mood and thought the suggestion was ridiculous.

They were not discouraged at all by my bad attitude and began a Google search that led them to Saint Maria Gemma Umberta Galgani. She had died in 1903 and was an Italian mystic, venerated as St. Gemma in the Roman Catholic Church since 1940. Among her patronages are paratroopers and parachutists and those suffering back injury or back pain. Paratroopers and parachutists must have bad backs too. All that landing impact, perhaps? It didn't matter. What did matter was now I had a saint on my side. St. Gemma was another guardian angel on my team, there to provide comfort and support.

I immediately ordered Saint Gemma medals (basically like baseball trading cards for Catholics) and began telling everyone I knew about Saint Gemma. I made sure to send one of the medals to my Benedictine sister Monica before her fusion. This was going to be the piece of encouragement I should share with others and, on the hard days, with myself.

I worked on being grateful for my body even though I felt betrayed by it. I worked on having compassion for myself and then looked for ways to show kindness to my friends and family. I'm that person that wants to see progress. What can I do today? What small steps can I accomplish that, no matter how trivial, will make me better? So I found ways to show up each day, whether that was returning one email, calling up a friend, standing up from a chair without fear, or putting one dish in the dishwasher.

If I got too in my head with worries about my future, I gently reminded myself to be in the moment. I didn't know what the future held, so I had to believe this pain wouldn't last forever. I had to learn to live moment to moment again and to take advantage and be grateful for the few times I could get comfortable or had the energy to get things done in preparation for my trip back to Mayo. I had to believe there were going to be better days. Otherwise, what is there to live for? I had to reframe the narrative.

I stopped playing the what-if-game and tried to make peace with what had happened and the tough road ahead. I went through an ego mourning of what could have been if my back didn't break a second time. I reread my inspiring books and found a few new ones. I cranked up my fight songs, even if it was just to walk around the house. I tried to adapt to my new situation to persevere and not throw in the towel. I had to listen to my body and practice silencing my inner critic. All the same steps that had guided me the first go-round were my lifesavers again.

Hope Nugget: When shit hits the fan, don't go down the blame bandwagon, but find a wall to lean on, remembering that this situation is bigger than just you. The lessons you'll discover may not even be for you.

Chapter 7

Another Walk at Dawn

*G*roundhog Day.

It was time to do it all again. I flew to my mom's home in Des Moines on the fifteenth of November, and she and I drove to Mayo on the seventeenth for a plethora of imaging and meetings with my surgeon and his team. It was surreal to walk into that beautiful lobby again with the floor-to-ceiling windows, and every wood and glass surface polished and sparkling. I was as moved as I had been the first time by the gorgeous music coming from the grand piano but felt like I was living my own personal *Groundhog Day* movie with me, the unwilling star, playing the lead instead of Bill Murray.

Mom and I were on autopilot in the same hotel, eating the same PB&J sandwiches again and chuckling together. I was always worried about the stress I was putting on her, but she never complained or said a negative thing. She assured me she was happy to help and pleased to be needed and with me one hundred percent of the way.

There were two differences this time around though.

One: We now had Saint Gemma medals with us. Two: My angel of a sister, Carol, volunteered to make the trek to Rochester to be with us, and arrived the day before my surgery so Mom wouldn't have to be alone on the day of my surgery. Spinal fusions were known to last eight to nine hours and I know Mom would be constantly worrying. I was so grateful Carol would be there to distract her and to keep her company. That fact alone gave me the peace I needed to prepare for surgery.

I was encouraged after meeting with my team and my surgeon, Dr. Paul Huddleston. That old fear that I was unfixable melted away when he said, "We're going to Henneberry-proof your back." Yes! That was just the message I needed to hear.

Friends had been texting me all day, making sure I never felt alone, and I was beyond appreciative for their support. Then, I received a message from Melinda, my yoga master. She sent me a link to the song "O-o-h Child" by the Five Stairsteps. I hadn't heard that song in years, but it was a perfect choice and filled me with even more thankfulness. The song promises that things will get easier, days will be brighter, and that we'll all walk in the beautiful sun together once more. With the song playing on repeat, I walked down the hall where cancer patients were receiving treatment. I looked into the eyes of so many beautiful women in their unique designs of head wraps. I felt appreciated as I smiled at each one in turn and wished they could hear the song too.

We were each experiencing extreme trials, but I had to choose faith, not just for me, but for them. I felt a deep kinship with these women who both humbled and inspired me, and so for the rest of the day, with "O-o-h Child" cranked loud in my ear drums, I sent along a silent message to each patient I passed: *We will walk in the rise of the beautiful sun. We have to be brave and believe.*

It was the nineteenth of November as I found myself awake at dawn and trudging through the deserted, snowy Rochester streets to my third surgery. The difference this time was that I wasn't on my own. Carol had offered to drive me to the hospital, but I told her my claim to fame was that I walked to my spinal surgeries. It was kind of a badass thing to do, and it helped me get in warrior mode for surgery. When I refused the drive, Carol insisted on walking the trek with me so here we were.

The path felt so eerily familiar, but the joy of having my sister next to me was what took hold of me. I knew the first two weeks of recovery would suck, but I was ready to face it and make my first baby steps to a new life, hopefully one without pain or limitations. I cranked up my fight songs for our walk, and we smiled and sang along. Even though I was starting the journey anew, I felt grateful that I was fixable and that I wasn't alone. I allowed the hope that this would be my last surgery to propel me forward.

THE POWER OF THE MAYO WAY

It was eleven at night, and I was lying in my recovery room with my eyes open, unable to sleep. The surgery had gone well, and they had successfully refused my spine with the cobalt equipment. Still, I couldn't help but feel anxious.

Would this fusion work? Would this all be worth it someday? Would I ever be able to be my old self again?

As if he could sense I needed someone, Dr. Huddleston walked into my room and placed a warm blanket, fresh out of the dryer, over my body. Ah, the heat was so soothing, and my body instantly relaxed with this feeling that I was safe. I loved that he didn't even ask but knew the warmth would soothe me. It was that priceless moment that the Mayo Clinic always did so well, a moment where you feel genuinely cared for and not just data on a chart or money to an insurance company.

He was still in his scrubs with his face mask pulled down. My surgery began at five thirty a.m., and it looked like I was his last stop on a busy and long day. Though I was exhausted, my first thought was to worry about his health. He had to be wiped in every way. He never gave any signs that he was though, and instead surprised me by asking a question.

"Pat, are there any lessons you've learned that I could learn? Or lessons that could help others going through this surgery?"

I was honored and, once again, felt seen and validated. I answered with the first thing that came to mind. "I think people need to stay healthy because this can come out of nowhere. I don't think I would have survived three surgeries if I hadn't lived a healthy lifestyle before my back first broke. I was strong physically after a life of exercise and healthy living, which helped me become strong mentally too."

"That's wonderful, Pat. Thank you."

As he left, I reflected on what an amazing head coach he was for his team and patients. I knew he'd never give up on me, and that gave me the courage to face the numerous days of recovery that laid before me.

———————

The next day, it was time to try my first walk again. I noticed Mom had put a Saint Gemma medal on the nightstand next to my hospital bed, and it gave me a sense of motivation, knowing a saint was looking out for me. A physical therapist was there to help me carefully get out of bed and latch on to my walker. I went into the hallway and was reminded of the embarrassment I felt the first time I did this with the last surgery. I couldn't fathom how hard it was to learn to walk again. I kept my head down and focused on each baby step with all the determination I could muster.

With my head down though, I was trapped in the internal loop of only paying attention to my pain. Pain is a tempting companion, but it aims to drag you down if you give too much of yourself over to it. Thus, though I was doing my hallway walk each day, by the third day I hadn't improved much.

In such a circumstance, painkillers are always offered. Many times, they can be helpful, but this time I specifically told the nurses not to give me any.

"But, Pat, they will help you *want* to get up and walk."

"You don't know me. I will always want to get up and walk," I retorted. I didn't want a crutch, even if it would be helpful.

On day one of my recovery, I'd noticed outside my room a young boy walking down the hallway in a halo traction brace with weights and metal surrounding his head. He must have been ten years old, and Mayo had given him a doctor's badge and scrubs to wear. On the second and third day, I noticed him again. Before I could get out of bed, I would watch him walk down the hall, and I couldn't wait to meet him. In my head I referred to him as "Dr. Halo."

On the fourth day of my recovery, I decided to begin timing my walks so we'd meet. As I approached him, I stopped and asked, "How are rounds today, Doctor?"

He looked me straight in the eye, became very serious, and said, "I'll be checking in on your case." It took everything in me not to laugh. Instead, I just smiled and said, "Thank you, Doctor. I appreciate that." His serious look upturned into a big, heart melting grin before he continued on.

For my remaining time at Mayo, I timed my walk when he was making his rounds. I realized in our first meeting that he had a learning disability and he reminded me of one of my swimmers on my Special Olympics swim team. He always made me smile on my walks and gave me something to look forward to each day. I woke up every morning not wanting to miss the rounds of this young Dr. Halo.

What stood out to me most was how strong and confident he was when he walked down the hallway, even with these weights coming down and surrounding him in steel. He was serious about checking in on patients and did so with a wholehearted mantra that caring for others was his purpose there. What I loved the most is that Mayo let him be what he needed to be. They permitted him to walk up and down the hallway with his badge and scrubs to help with his journey. Each day as we finished our conversation, he would look me in the eyes and say, "You're doing a good job!" It was heart-healing medicine.

I began to take his mantra on for myself. I stopped looking down and started to not care about how I appeared to others as much. I began to notice how those around me were doing. I saw how the cheerleaders around me—my mom, the nurses, doctors, and the other patients—were all struggling too. I started keeping my head lifted, smiling at the people I passed, and thus, began to recognize others. I cherished the connections and used it as fuel to go just a bit farther each day. If I made even an ounce of improvement, that would be a victory for my entire team. Walking down hallways with eyes open was good morale for us all.

One week into my recovery, my sister met a family whose elderly mother had the same surgery. She was one day post-op, and was scared to try and walk, and even more terrified that she would never be herself again. One week out, I wasn't sure I had enough perspective to offer her any hope, but I stopped by her room.

I could see the fear in her eyes as I listened to her state how she was doing. She worried about being a burden to her family, she worried if this was the beginning of the end of her life, she worried if she was going to be stuck in a wheelchair for the rest of her days, if her independence would evaporate. As we chatted, it was as if the compassion I had received from Mayo was fuel for the compassion I felt for this woman. I stayed for about thirty minutes, and when it was time for me to leave, I shared with her my simple discovery.

"I'm a week out, and I feel okay and am walking with the walker. Every day you're going to get better and stronger. My one piece of advice is don't have your head down when you walk. Lift up your eyes. You'll see how that makes it easier to walk a little farther every day."

No More Hospitals

It was two weeks after my surgery, and I wanted to leave Mayo a little early because we found out a gigantic snowstorm was on the way. When a Midwesterner says a gigantic snowstorm is coming, they mean one of epic proportions. We're talking fifty MPH winds, blowing snow so hard you can't see your hand in front of your face. We're talking twenty feet high snow drifts. We're talking you have to get the heck out of dodge or be trapped until it's over. My sister and mom had already been in a hotel for two weeks, and I couldn't fathom them staying longer than was necessary. The storm was predicted to be a doozy, and if we didn't leave now, they would be stuck in the hotel, and I would have to remain at Mayo for another whole week at least.

My insurance company wanted me to go to rehab for a few weeks as I was a "fall risk,' but it was going to take the insurance "time" to officially approve that move, and I didn't have time to wait. My Mayo team knew my determination and were leaning toward letting me go as long as I could make it through their checklist proving I could do things somewhat independently. I had to show that I could step up and down from a block they placed in front of me. Then I had to prove I could get in and out of a car correctly with this fake car they had in the rehab facility. With my condition, there were particular ways of getting in and out of a car. Five years ago, if you would've told me I would be in physical therapy to learn how to get out of a car, I would've thought that sounded like the most ridiculous thing. Oh, how we are humbled! The main obstacle I had to overcome though was showing my team that I could get from Point A to Point B using my walker. I crushed that (well, if you consider a snail's

91

pace while you are constantly reminding yourself not to get the walker too far away from your body crushing it).

The team told me my recovery would be similar to the first surgery but would probably take longer since a second surgery was more trauma on my body. I would need to commit to a plan and do my exercises every day. I agreed and, though I didn't really have an astute plan, Mayo reluctantly approved my discharge home. I left the hospital that day with my mom and Carol, and we bolted out of Rochester as carefully and quickly as my newly fused back could take.

Halfway home, I got a call from my insurance company saying I'd finally been approved to go to a rehab hospital. As I hung up the phone, I told my mom and sister, "I don't want to go there. Keep driving!" As the words came out of my mouth, I looked at my mom for her approval. I knew that by going home, I was putting more stress on her to make meals, watch over me, and do those intimate things I couldn't do for myself. She didn't even hesitate.

"Do what *you* want to do," was my mom's simple reply.

I don't recommend this to anyone, and please follow your medical professionals' advice, but in a year and a half, I'd been in seven hospitals and was over it. To go back again to another hospital for rehab was the breaking point for me. I knew how to rehab at home from my first surgery, and felt it was the perfect place for me to work on becoming stronger, both physically and mentally, than I was before the surgery. And if this idea turned out to be stupid, well then, I could always go back to a rehab hospital. But first I needed to trust my gut.

I settled into my seat with relief, knowing I was going home. I stared out the window at the snowy freeways that we blurred past and prayed a heap of gratitude. I thanked God for my mom and my sister being here with me, for Mayo and my surgeon, for the resiliency of my body, and for the fact that I had survived a second fusion. I sighed and closed my eyes, and as I did, I couldn't help wondering, *What else does the universe have planned for me?*

Hope Nugget: Lift up your eyes. You'll see how that makes it easier to walk a little farther every day.

Part Two

The Comeback

Chapter 8

Basement Walking

Forty-four. That's how many steps it takes to get from one side of my mom's basement to the other side. It is a number I never expected to know so fully, but no matter how fast or slow I walked, the number stayed the same. Forty-four steps to one side, take a moment to catch my breath, do an about-face, and trek to the other side. Forty-four more. A friend told me once that the number forty-four is supposed to represent the spiritual message of knowing your guardian angels are beside you. I worked hard to remember that in the moments where all I wanted to do was give up, frustrated that walking forty-four steps still produced a struggle.

The main thing the doctors told me to do post-surgery was to walk every day, and it was explained to me that the more I walked during those first few months of recovery, the better off I would be. Though my soul cringed with the fact that I was in recovery again, I knew the key would be consistency more than anything, and I would follow their advice. Thus, with a Midwestern winter roaring outside, I was sentenced to workouts in the basement. Forty-four steps.

In my childhood, mom's basement was *the* hangout spot. When friends came over, we'd be chilling down there playing board games, dancing to records, and competing in very serious ping pong matches. So many of my memories take place in that basement, and they hit me as I deemed this space my new rehabilitation center.

This was quite different from my last rehab center post fusion number one. Here, as I stepped one slow step at a time across the basement, I was overwhelmed with nostalgia. I stepped past our ping-pong table, still there, but the net had mostly fallen apart and had to be held up with clothespins. I walked past our old Christmas tree in the corner. I grew up decorating that thing with tinsel, sparkly balls, and a varied mosaic of meaningful ornaments including a few popsicle stick angels my sisters and I had made one year. Next to the tree were shelves that held old white cigar boxes with lids (my grandfather had loved cigars). Those cigar boxes held treasures too sacred for me to open—letters written between my mom and dad during the Korean War. I could never bring myself to read those letters, but I did once read a letter my grandfather had written to my dad. In the letter he'd praised my father for how much money he was sending home from his time in the Army, and how he should have saved enough by the time he got back to buy a decent car. He was sending back eighteen dollars at a time, and I mused on how my father might've been encouraged by such a letter, knowing his time away from Mom would have some rewards.

I paused in my walk as I passed rustic golf clubs that belonged to my dad, tempted to pull a nine iron out and use it as a cane. Next to the clubs were Mom's old ice skates atop a few boxes, which seemed an inappropriate place. They should be in a fancy display case labeled *"The belongings of a Saint."* Dad's war boots were beside her skates, and I wondered if his legs ever felt as shaky as mine do now when he wore those. They must have.

I couldn't help but think of my childhood during these walks and wonder what young Pat would think of me now. Young Pat, who dreamed big and never slowed down and met each day with joy and hunger and motivation. Oh, and such easy movement. She knew how to strengthen her body to get the most out of it. She believed there were limits she would break, and records to do outdo, and she loved having those goals. She never allowed fear to be her guide. How I yearned to be able to move freely, to pick up ice skates and go out in the frozen tundra and skate. Or to even feel that natural hope for a second. Or to dream without boundaries. Instead, I replayed my past because I was too afraid to see my future. I felt like if young Pat were to meet me in that basement now, she'd have no idea who I was. That thought terrified me.

I did another forty-four steps and shed some tears. Forty-four more and took a multitude of deep, long breaths. The tears dried. I couldn't let terror reign.

Second chances tend to have a positive connotation. Those two words flood my brain with images of great underdog victories, resiliency lessons, and inspiring comeback tales. Second chances are full of hope, healing, and forgiveness. There are so many opportunities for second chances, and I think, as humans, we often forget that and paralyze ourselves with the fear of making that first mistake. I've learned though that making that first mistake can teach you far more than never taking a risk. I've also learned that more often than not, grace can be found in the midst of these blunders, making you wonder just what you were afraid of to begin with. All the sports I loved gave me second chances. You are allowed two false starts in swimming. In tennis, you have two tries to serve the ball. In baseball, you get three strikes. They could just give you one, but having multiple attempts means that when you make that first error, there is still a chance for you to redeem yourself. Second chances are beautiful.

Except when you don't want them.

Here I was, having a second chance at a spinal fusion recovery and boy did I hate that fact. I didn't need a second chance at this. I'd already suffered so much and had tried my best to do good with the lessons I had learned. Was that not enough? What else could I gain from this?

I wished my brain could've summoned up a positive spin, encouraging myself to do recovery better this time. How could I be more disciplined this time? How could I usher forth more compassion this time? How could I use my story to help others this time? But more often than not, I was a wreck, far away from seeing any potential good in this situation and cursing the truth that I had to do this all over again. I was still bitter that not one doctor, nurse, physical therapist, or Facebook support group ever mentioned even the possibility that the rods and screws in a fusion could break. Here I was the impossible warrior, the experiment, the woman whose hardware broke so that she would have the beautiful opportunity to do it all over again. Lucky me. Ugh.

To my mother's dismay, I often stayed locked away, using the basement as a shield, and uttering an ever-increasing heap of f-bombs that made me want to wash my own mouth out with soap. My mind often spiraled until I didn't recognize the voice in my head. I was unemployed, crippled, away from the community I'd built in Austin, and depressed. I hated my life.

What I needed was a comeback.

Who doesn't love an amazing comeback story? The most exciting games to watch are those when a team is down by a significant margin and yet somehow manages to slide their way back into victory right before the clock expires. I've always choked up when I hear any story of an athlete who was supposed to have a career ending injury and yet found a way to get back in their sport after a remarkable recovery. What always appealed to me most in these stories is not just that these people came back, but that they came back *stronger*.

I wasn't sure what a comeback could look like in my state. What did I need to learn to get through this? A comeback might be just getting through it. A comeback, maybe, was really not about going back, but about understanding something bigger.

While recovering at Mom's, I was reminded of one of my favorite comeback stories: the story of Diana Nyad. She was a long-distance swimming icon in the 1970s who accomplished multiple world records for such feats as circling Manhattan Island in record time and swimming from The Bahamas to Florida. After her Bahamas to Florida swim, she retired from swimming in the public eye and worked for thirty years as a sports journalist and broadcaster.

In 2011, her mother passed away, and a dream rekindled in her. She remembered being a child with her mother in

Florida, and her mom pointing out Cuba to her and saying it looked so close that you could swim there. It was a term of expression more than a truth, but a piece of Diana had always held onto that possibility. She had tried it once in the '70s but had trouble swimming in a shark cage and a storm had veered her so off course that she had to call it quits. Now felt like the perfect time. She was sixty and reflecting on her life, and she knew she wasn't done. She had more to prove, and though her body wasn't the same as in her thirties, her mental strength was ten times stronger. She needed to do this.

In September 2013 at the age of sixty-four, after multiple failed attempts (aka near death experiences), Diana Nyad became the first person to swim from Havana, Cuba to Key West, Florida, a distance of 111 miles, without a shark cage. What a badass!

Having remembered this story, I decided to read more about it and landed on Diana's website. There was a quote at the top of her bio page from D.L. Stewart of the *Dayton Daily News*, which stated, "The toughest athlete in the world is a 62-year-old woman."[1]

I was approaching sixty, and as I read that I got chills up and down my fused-together spine. I knew it was no coincidence that this story had popped into my life again. Diana's story was my sign that it is never too late to begin again.

A couple months before the rods and screws broke, I was asked by my friend Alissa Magrum to participate in an

---

1. http://diananyad.com/diana/

annual open water swim benefit for the organization she was the Executive Director for called *Colin's Hope*. In 2008, four-year-old Colin Holst tragically drowned in a public swimming pool that was equipped with lifeguards and family members present. Colin's parents learned that drowning was the number one cause of accidental deaths for children under five[2], and they used their grief to fuel a mission to help others. *Colin's Hope* is a phenomenal organization that provides resources and training on drowning prevention. As a long-time friend of Alissa, I knew about this non-profit since their inception. I love their mission and encourage everyone to check out and donate to their amazing cause.

Alissa consistently invited me to volunteer for all sorts of amazing causes, and though I'd always been gung-ho to participate in anything Alissa asked me to (she is one of those go-getters you always want on your team), and had participated in this event numerous times before, I was nervous about swimming long distances in my current condition. I was about eight months into my recovery post first fusion, and still very cautious about what my body could or couldn't do. That being said, this year the open water swim would be done as a team relay so the distance that I'd need to swim would be less than it had been in the past.

As I debated what to do, I remembered how Alissa had visited me in the hospital at the beginning of this journey, handing me that *"Trust the Process"* T-shirt, and making me write down goals on the whiteboard when I was in such a desperate state. One of those goals had been to participate in

2. https://www.colinshope.org/

the *Colin's Hope* open water swim again. When I realized that, I knew I had to try this.

I let Alissa know, and her first reaction was, "Yes, Pat! This is amazing! This will be your comeback swim!"

I should've met her with enthusiasm and agreed with her. I should've been excited to test my limits and go out there and give it my all, even in my current circumstances. I should've.

Instead, I was immediately repelled by what she said. This could *not* be my comeback swim. I was far too weak, too out of practice, and too scared of even participating in this for it to be my comeback swim. I didn't feel ready for a comeback, and thus I let her words go to the wayside.

Interestingly enough, I was right in knowing that the event wasn't my comeback swim. Eight weeks later my rods and screws broke, and any thoughts of comebacks would have to be put on hold.

I wondered now, a couple months post second fusion, what I wanted my comeback to look like. I was realizing that part of coming back stronger would be accepting my new normal and allowing myself time to heal after each setback. Notice I say *accepting* but not defining. We are more than the limitations of our bodies. I would have to believe that. Could I come back stronger physically than I was before my surgeries? No, my body was put through the life-altering ringer. Could I come back stronger mentally than I was before my surgeries? Possibly. And the fact that it was possible was what I would need to hold onto.

Hope Nugget: We are more than our limitations. Hold on to the possibilities.

Chapter 9

New Dreams

My skates made their initial contact with the ice, and the scratching noise alerted me to home in my focus on what needed to be my best performance yet. I skated into my starting position with my toe pointing to the left complete with my opposite arm raised up high in an elegant stance. Classical music began playing, my cue to start, and I tuned out the noise of the crowd and focused solely on my routine.

The rink was mine and I took up the space, cruising around with figure eights, pivots, hops, and crossovers. I channeled my inner ballerina, molding my arms expressively, using them as both creative choices and to help with my balance. As the music got bolder, so did my moves. I shimmied my shoulders and then prepared for and landed a loop jump. I glided to the center and did my flashy step sequence, followed by a flying sit spin. As I came up, I grabbed my right leg and pulled it up until my foot was far above my head. My entire core shook, but I was determined to not show it. My routine was almost done.

So far I hadn't fallen, but I tried to keep such a thought

out of my head as I prepared for the final move. I increased my speed, geared up my faith, and completed a triple axel, landing firmly, the ice skidding beneath my blades. Yes! With a smile, I skated into my final pose raising both my arms up in the air.

The crowd roared and now I could let them in. I skated off the rink and waited for the judges scores. The announcement came, and boldly through the arena was an excited voice stating, "Pat Henneberry has won the gold medal!" I burst into a shocked smile and tears. My dream finally came true.

I was ten years old when I imagined this scenario. The 1972 Winter Olympics were taking place in Sapporo, Japan, and each night I would grab my dad's transistor radio, which he had won from A Metropolitan Life Insurance sales contest and walk down to our frozen pond. There was one wooden lamp post by the pond that shone brightly on the ice. I would turn on the radio, tuning the station to the one which was airing the Olympics, and step onto the ice. The pond cracked under my feet as more of it began freezing and expanding. Then, as I listened to the commentators describe the routines of the figure skaters, I would imagine myself as them. I would boldly dream that I would someday be an Olympic skater.

The next night the event might be speed skating so I would switch gears from figure skating to speed skating and see how fast I could cross the pond and back. Nobody ever came by or bothered me out there on that frozen pond. It was just me and the radio training for the Olympics.

In 1976, I was fourteen and this time the Winter

Olympics were held in Innsbruck, Austria. I took on the same routine, grabbing that radio each night, and walking down to the pond to focus on my dreams.

As an adult, I couldn't help but still get sucked into the Olympics, my imagination thrilling me as I put myself in the skates of the athletes I watched on TV. I was always inspired by them, and watching their greatness ignited some core belief that I could achieve something great too.

In 2002, the Winter Olympics were being held in Salt Lake City, Utah. My best friend Anne was given two tickets to the Olympics by her client John Hancock Financial, who was one of the sponsors of the Winter Olympics, and she invited *me* to go along! I couldn't believe it. To actually witness the Olympics in person was an absolute dream come true! The John Hancock team treated us like gold, making sure we got tickets to the gold medal hockey game, gold medal figure skating, and speed skating events.

One of the activities at the Olympics is pin trading. A tradition that's been around for hundreds of years and involves pins from around the world representing different countries, Olympic events, or even specific moments from the Olympics. Anne's client gave each of us ten pins to start with, and then the game was on to collect more or to trade for better, more unique pins.

You would display the pins on your bag or hat or clothing, and automatically they would be a conversation starter. It was an amazing way to meet people from all over the world. Thankfully, I was in sales, so I was all about this and grew quite the collection. I had a strategic capacity to trade one pin for two or three.

One of my favorite pins was a *Happy St. Patrick's Day* pin that had a big Irish shamrock and the Olympic rings on it. I had an American flag pin that rotated to reveal the Olympic Rings as well. I had a bobsled team pin, and an ice-skating pin where a figure skate actually moved. There was an amazing Kodak 1998 pin with a photo of gold medalist Tara Lipinski ice skating. One of my most valuable pins was a Twin Towers pin. 9/11 had just happened a few months prior, and I was able to trade a bunch of pins in exchange for that one.

One of the days, while having lunch, Marie Osmond came up to me to trade pins and we ended up having a full on forty-five-minute conversation about our pins. I loved that so many people took this fun idea of pin trading so seriously. In my heart, I vowed to come back to the Olympics someday with all my pins in tow.

That conversation with Marie was a blast, but the most memorable moment of the Olympics happened on a day when we had some down time. The hotel we were staying at had an outside ice-skating rink and, knowing that I had brought my ice skates, I went down to the rink, laced up my skates, and began skating these wonderful figure eights my mom had taught me when I was a kid.

I wasn't the only one on the rink, and after a few minutes of being out there a woman skated up behind me and said, "Wow, you've been taught by one of the best."

To this I answered, "Well, my mother was an amazing figure skater and us kids were all taught to skate the correct way, before we could even walk."

The correct way meant that Mom had never given us any crutches when we learned. We never used a double-bladed skate or had someone with a chair in front of us on the ice in case we fell. She made sure from the start that we had perfect form.

As I looked up from my skating to see who was talking to me, I almost ate it. It was Peggy Fleming. Freaking Olympic Gold medalist Peggy Fleming. She also happened to be my mom's favorite figure skater of all time.

For the next hour, Peggy and I skated around the rink and talked. She was amazingly kind, authentic, and down to earth. When we finished skating, I couldn't help myself as I knew it would bring my mom so much joy, and asked Peggy if she'd mind saying hi to mom really quick on the phone. She agreed, and so I called my mom.

"Hi, Mom. I'm out skating, and I want someone to say hi to you." I handed the phone over.

"Hi, Marion. This is Peggy Fleming."

How my mom kept her cool I will never know, but for the next thirty minutes Marion Henneberry and Peggy Fleming chatted on the phone like old friends, debating over whether Michelle Kwan or Sarah Hughes would win the gold medal that night.

I was forty years old when I skated with Peggy Fleming, and that night, as I watched the women's gold medal figure skating event (Sarah Hughes took home the gold), I was still dreaming of what it would be like to be one of them. All night, happiness bubbled over in me, knowing that my ten-year-old self was still there, cuddled up inside me.

Keep On Dreaming

Post second fusion, I was struggling to dream. I was warped by both the fear of falling and the fear of failing, and it hindered any dream that tiptoed into my heart. So many of the things I loved to do I would most likely not be able to do again. Would it even be worth it to dream again, knowing there was the possibility of those dreams being ripped away from me in an instant too?

My dreams had always felt so real to me, and it scared me to not recognize myself in my inability to imagine a better future for myself. As I sat with this unfamiliarity, I realized that if I was going to forge a comeback, I would have no choice but to remember how to dream.

Being such a competitor and athlete helped me dive into the rollercoaster of recovery. I was used to having good swims and bad swims. Days where the runner's high came easy and times when it was a struggle to beat yesterday's distance. After two spinal fusions, I looked back and thought about how easy-going it was to train for a trail hike or open water swim. Had a bad day? No worries, you just attack that goal again the next day.

It's much harder to gather your strength for multiple years in and out of physical therapy. How boring is that? I've always been someone who is jetting around the world for work or having an amazingly filled social calendar. My life was beginning to feel like a hamster on a wheel, endlessly running with no purpose, or like I'd been on the *Polar Express* train for months without knowing where I was going. I would tell myself that *ultimately, the train has to go somewhere, right?* But nothing felt like it was moving forward.

When I harped on this idea of a comeback, I realized I needed new goals. I was learning that resiliency isn't about focusing on the wheel, but focusing on what the commitment you make to keep going is doing in you—mind, body, and soul. What helps to see beyond the wheel is to set new goals to get out of the muck and unstuck both emotionally and physically.

My new goals would have to be realistic while paired with a reach. Some would have to be practical, and some would have to be wild. Unfortunately, I felt so awkward and unsure in my new self. *What is too much for me to handle? What is the measuring stick for success? How can I be gracious with my body, but also lovingly push it further?* I was overwhelmed with differing thoughts when I first sat down to write down new goals, but eventually I boiled down the list to these two questions:

1. What do I want to achieve?
2. What's an attainable goal that will still push me?

I knew I might make mistakes in over/underestimating my ability, but I had to stay committed to pushing toward something brighter in my future. So I began writing out some ideas:

- Pick up pickleball.
- Go to happy hour with friends once a month.
- Add one *new* physical therapy exercise a week to spice things up.
- Get strong enough to attend the next annual National Park trail hike with the crew.
- Get a dog.
- Write a book.
- Become a professional speaker.
- Take a vacation this year.
- Go to Las Olas surf camp.

A few years ago, I heard about the incredible Las Olas surf camp for women. Their mission statement emphasizes that *"We make girls out of women."* I loved that, and I loved surfing, having done it a few times on vacation in Costa Rica and Hawaii. I had always craved to do it more. When I found a holistic week-long retreat that specialized in beginner surf lessons designed specifically for women and their bodies at any age, but also tied in yoga, meditation, positive mindset training, and a whole lot of play on the sands of a gorgeous Mexican beach town, I was all in. I rarely took vacations, but this was just the thing that would encourage me to do so.

I began the inquiry process and settled in on a week in May that would work perfectly with my schedule. This was going to be the retreat I always dreamed of, and I couldn't wait! That is until my initial back incident took place a few weeks later.

A year into recovery from my first fusion, I desperately needed something to look forward to, so I contacted the retreat again. In my email, I wrote, *"My dream is to go to this retreat. A year ago, I was planning on signing up, but the Universe had other plans and instead had to opt for a spinal fusion surgery. I'm a year into my recovery and I know I couldn't physically carry the surfboard or get up on the board by myself, but if I had help, I know that once I'm in the water I'm a really strong swimmer and would be okay. I am planning on getting my legs strong enough to stand up on a board through Pilates, yoga, and physical therapy, and am confident that once I am standing up on a board, I'll be able to stay there for a bit. I want to do everything I can to have this experience and to be up on a board surfing!"*

They responded with so much love stating that it would be no problem for me to join; that they were a supportive group that would love to help me in the pursuit of this dream of mine. My giddiness took off as I imagined myself, fused back and all, up on a surfboard in warm, tropical waters.

Unfortunately, just as my luck would have it, a month later the rods in my spine broke and I was summoned back to surgery. I was heartbroken that Las Olas would have to wait once more, but I haven't given up hope that someday I'll be there, and the timing will be perfect.

My dreams post fusions are vastly different than before, but they aren't any less important. In fact, they feel even more important somehow. When I was in the hospital for weeks on end, making a list of future plans was the only thing that kept me sane. On the darkest nights of my soul, the fantasies I had for my future self gave me a resiliency to face the next day head-on. I told myself that *on the other side of misery and sacrifice, there must be a reward worth everything.*

The fact that I could dream meant my story wasn't over yet. It meant there are still unknown adventures for me to partake in, and more beautiful surprises than I can imagine. I felt a thrill knowing there were new friends to be made, lessons to be learned, and a new self to love better than I ever have. I knew I may not be able to swing a tennis racquet at ninety years old, but I hoped I'd be able to slay on the pickle-ball court. I committed to dreaming of falling in love and finding that long life partner who will shock me with how great of a match we are. I made goals of traveling the world again and of speaking to groups of people with messages of hope, resiliency, and courage. I aimed to turn my story into a book! That was a huge dream of mine. And I prayed that this book would inspire others to live their life to the fullest no matter what they are going through. Whatever adventures life had in store for me, I would remember that the lessons learned and the bravery that might be born, had all the potential to make me stronger.

P.S. My hope for any of you reading this is that if at this moment there is something clawing at you that you want to do–a dream, a hope, a vision, a bucket list item–then please stop reading this book right now and go do it! Start walking, painting, volunteering, going to a surf camp, taking up a sport, or learning how to clog (my good friend Zoe is a great clogger and I've wanted to clog like her). Look for a community to join, whether for movie lovers, aspiring chefs, or environmental enthusiasts who volunteer to pick up trash off the beach. Make today count and use the blessing of health (wherever you're at on that spectrum) to be playful and adventurous.

Hope Nugget: Dreaming is what will get you through the muck. No matter what season you are in, keep on dreaming so that you remember to *live*.

Chapter 10

The Loneliness Precipice

W hen I walked through my door on that day in April and felt my leg was about to explode, I thought that the searing pain was my number one tormentor. Turns out that isolation can be just as agonizing. From the first night of my injury through my first two surgeries and rehab, I was shocked to find that my loneliness was almost more unbearable than my injury. It multiplied my suffering by one thousand percent.

I had hard nights alone in my bedroom. I had even longer nights in the Austin hospitals, Mayo Clinic, and rehab facilities I was sent to. Those first three weeks in hospitals, the loneliness was unbearable, and the physical agony fueled my heartache. Even when a friend would visit me in the hospital, eventually, they would leave. Once the door closes, you are alone with only your thoughts and fears.

I felt sorry for myself and kept thinking of the family I should've had, the kids I could have adopted, and all the bucket list items I hadn't accomplished yet. Why did this happen to me? How is it that I have no one to call "my person?" Though I'm blessed to have so many people say they love me, I laid there overwhelmed with loneliness. Of course, people love me, but why isn't anyone *in love* with me? How can I be in this place? I can't move, I can't dress myself, I can't walk. Shit.

Knowing that I didn't have "that person," a partner, someone who would help me make decisions and be there for me no matter what weighed on me. Yes, I was crazy fortunate to have my mom, caring friends, family, and neighbors, and they would be there at the drop of a hat. But there was an intimacy I was craving, a hole that hadn't been filled, and a point person I yearned for my team. As I sat in those medical facilities, the truth bared its ugly face, and I knew I was lonely long before my injury. Loneliness had been lurking around the corner for years.

Obsessing over that thought fueled many nights of lying in my hospital bed alone, crying, and saying my thousand Hail Mary's. Sometimes a crisis forces you to see all the wounds you've been running away from. Nurses would come into my room and ask if they could call someone for me. I knew they meant well by this sweet gesture, but my answer was always no. I didn't want to wake anyone. My family had work to get to the next morning. Many of my friends didn't even know I was here. Everyone else had their own big lives to deal with. The last thing they needed was for sleep to be taken from them because of my problems.

I've always been able to adapt and move forward. I've always felt I can survive anything. But I've never been good at asking for help and I've always been afraid of dying alone. Having spent many years traveling internationally for my career, I had this on-going fear that I would die in a hotel, and no one would find me for days. I never thought that the monster of pain and loneliness would kill me in my own house, but now I was imagining such an ordeal. Fear spun a frightening story in my head where I had no future. All I had were questions: *Who would want to be with me now that I'm broken? Who will take care of me if I can't take care of myself? How can I continue if every day hurts this much?*

Because my world shifted in one day, I missed my community of friends and neighbors and had to find connections where I could. We're social animals and have a primal need to feel we belong no matter where we are. This is especially true whenever you're in the hospital or rehab.

I remember being at my first rehab facility in Austin, a few weeks after my fall, and I felt so isolated. I wanted to connect to someone. I wanted to feel belonging. Craving conversation and understanding, I reached out to the therapists and nurses who cheered me up when we talked. I loved figuring out the best questions to ask, and just sitting back and losing myself in listening to their stories. From complaining about the weather and their kids' soccer games to boyfriend troubles and funny stories of former patients, they thrilled me. It didn't have to be deep conversations as I learned that even the simplest of interactions lifted my spirits and got my head to think of something other than my injuries. They were all sweet and friendly but had jobs to do, and I could often sense a growing sense that they needed to be somewhere else while they were talking to me. Every time I noticed that, despite understanding that they were at work, I felt my disconnection grow.

I then turned to looking for connection as I walked down the halls, getting pleasure from just smiling at my fellow rehab patients. It wasn't easy, as many patients didn't have the strength to smile back at me, but forcing myself to smile made me feel better at least temporarily. On these walks I came to theorize that people don't like visiting hospitals because there's an air of separateness that is hard to shake. It's hard to build a community when everything feels unfamiliar, but maybe we humans just get in our own way.

An Unexpected Friend

After my first fusion, I was taken to a rehab hospital in Des Moines to help with the transition from surgery to recovery at home. Unfortunately, I hated the rehab hospital. The first night I got there, I heard blood curdling screaming on my floor and couldn't sleep. People were in so much pain there, and now I was one of them.

It was a huge recovery hospital, and you had the choice to have your meals in your room or in their large cafeteria. The nurses really encouraged everyone to have at least one meal in the cafeteria as it was good for working on movement and for social interaction. I knew that I would need assistance to go down to the cafeteria, and that fact depressed me, so I often wanted to stay in my room.

My mom came to visit me each day though, and with my mom at my side, I had the gumption to go to the cafeteria for lunch, enjoying the interaction with my mom. I noticed a woman, most likely in her 70s, that always ate by herself, but I didn't have it in me to go befriend her. I was still having trouble accepting that this was my reality, and I just wanted to hide from it all. Engaging with a stranger felt like too much, especially one who reminded me of suffering.

One day though, there was a snowstorm coming in and

my mom wouldn't be able to come see me. We talked on the phone and when she realized that without her, I had eaten lunch alone in my room, she encouraged me to go down to the cafeteria for dinner. I told her I wasn't up to it, but she kept pushing, and then my nurses also got on her side, and I was outnumbered. Fine, I would go eat dinner in the cafeteria.

On my way down, I thought of the woman who always ate by herself. I didn't know if she went down for dinner as well, but if so, I would make it a point to sit next to her so I wouldn't be alone. I could use some human connection, and my guess was she could too.

As the nurses helped me with my dinner selection and tray holding (walkers and holding dinner trays do not mesh well), I saw her sitting by herself. I let them know I wanted to sit next to her, and as we approached, I made sure to ask her, "Is it all right if I sit with you?"

She smiled and gave an affirmative nod. Her smile was infectious, and I matched it as I sat down beside her.

It didn't take long though to realize this woman couldn't talk. I would soon find out that she'd recently had a stroke, which took away her ability to talk and inhibited many of her motor functions. As I realized this, my first thought was, "Great, Pat! You finally had the nerve to sit with someone and talk, and you pick the one person who can't speak!"

But after a few minutes, I felt peace around her. Her smile said it all. There was no pressure to talk, which honestly was a gift, but if I had something I wanted to get off my chest, or a thought I hoped could encourage both of us, I would share it. She would listen intently, and I realized there are so many ways to communicate aside from words.

I began having my meals with her every day, and we

became friends. We'd pass each other in the halls and smile. Sometimes she would write me little notes, and I got to meet and know her family. They told me that before her stroke she had been a huge talker and always loved socializing with others. They thanked me for keeping her company, but truthfully, the company was mutual. She reminded me to keep lifting my eyes up, and to let people in.

CHRONIC PAIN

According to the Centers for Disease Control and Prevention, chronic pain affects over twenty percent of adults living in the United States[1]. Ugh. One in five of us are dealing with a pain that is absolutely relentless. It lives with you. It takes dignity from you. It feels like the devil is torturing you. The condition can even stump doctors, which on those days, you have no choice but to lock yourself in your room and pray for a miracle.

Chronic pain can also be a trickster. There are times where you can be feeling good for a day or two, or even a couple of weeks. When this happens hope gushes in. That is until the pain returns tenfold, almost like a game of peek-a-boo. Unfortunately, there is no giggling when the face of pain emerges. With the pain, you realize the hope you were feeling was a tease, and you wonder if what you felt was merely hope in disguise.

---

1. Dahlhamer J, Lucas J, Zelaya, C, et al. Prevalence of Chronic Pain and High-Impact Chronic Pain Among Adults — United States, 2016. MMWR Morb Mortal Wkly Rep 2018;67:1001–1006. DOI: http://dx.doi.org/10.15585/mmwr.mm6736a2external icon

In my comeback journey, I knew I needed to figure out a way to not let the pain define me. If it defines you then your existence feels hopeless. To do that I tried to separate myself from the pain almost like there are two people in the room— One who is in pain (my physical self) and one is looking at the other and encouraging perseverance (my mental self). Though the physical is real and important, we are so much more than our bodies. I couldn't forget that.

As someone who was taught to tough it out no matter what, I do my best to not show others I'm in pain. The truth is though, I am in pain most of the time, whether I make others aware of that or not. The silver lining is that I come to grow in my compassion for all people suffering with a chronic illness. To those battling with such a thing, I realize it doesn't always show. We may not notice how hard your body is working in order to do what most would think is a simple activity. We may not understand that every time you say yes to something, you are weighing the sacrifice your body will have to make for it. You overthink everything because you have to. You battle the physical, but you also battle the mental hoops that you are constantly working through. The physical impacts the mental and vice versa. Your body is tired, your brain is tired, and your soul is often exhausted. You want to shake others for complaining about their life when they can go through their day doing "normal things" with ease. You often want sympathy, but your illness might not be plastered on your forehead for all to see so people pass you on the street expecting you to do life at the speed of others. At the same time, you don't want others to think you are incapable. You don't want your boss to worry about giving you a promotion or your friends to not ask you for help when they need it. It's a cruel cycle wanting to be treated normally, but also needing moments where others realize you are not normal, and you require extra love and grace.

I know that when the pain is so bad that I can't help but limp, I am treated differently than the days where my pain is less showy. Though the days where I'm limping sound like they are worse, they aren't always. Sometimes the hardest days are the ones where no one sees what I'm going through, and I'm forced to convince others I need help. Asking a stranger to grab something for me because I can't get in the position to reach it when anyone would look at me and think I am perfectly able is not my favorite thing.

Please know that for those of you who are facing a similar mountain, whether it be physical or emotional or mental or spiritual, or all of the above, I see you. When you are struggling to convince others of the weight of your pain, know you aren't alone, and there *are* humans flowing with compassion who love you and want to understand. The greatest threat to all of us going through the ringer is to feel like no one could possibly understand. That just isn't true, and it encourages isolation, which is the most powerful tool in fueling despair. Fight against it if you can and find others in your life who can fight alongside you.

It has been the love from others that has helped me to see that I'm not done yet. Even with what feels like little to offer others, people still chose to show me kindness, to laugh and cry with me, to believe in a better future for me, and to show up with a heart ready to serve me. Though it's humbling for me to be in a position where I need help, it also wows me on the daily. People are so amazing, and their beautiful souls have forever impacted the way I will love others for the rest of my life.

For all of us going through this journey of pain, please know that our stories have so much more depth than we realize. When we allow others to help us, they become part of that story. They are learning and growing alongside us. Carry the motto yourself but allow others to remind you too: You are not done yet.

When I'm facing that precipice of a loneliness so scary, I think I can't shake it, I think about the divine. I think about all the prayers that have been said about me. I think about being created for a purpose. There are so many others in this world needing love, and I know I am capable of that. Then, I imagine loving future friends I have yet to meet, and I remember that no matter what, I am not alone.

Learning to Let Go

What old tape is running through your head that no longer serves you? That voice that tells you you're not good enough. When your world grows smaller and smaller as the agony takes over, what can you give up? What beliefs don't fit anymore? This is hard, soul-searching work, but were the questions I was asking myself during my recovery. I knew I needed to change my mental game if I was ever going to get on the other side of this.

Part of what separates us from others is the internal narrative we are believing about ourselves. This is why even if we are in a crowded room of people we love, we can only see our suffering and that suffering causes a distance and inability to make a connection outside of that suffering. *If I meet someone who doesn't understand me then they aren't worth my time.* How untrue is that! Though I've been guilty of such thinking, my goal has been to be better about learning from and then teaching the person whose life circumstances are different from my own.

Part of what I've been working on letting go of is the act of projecting my past onto my future. I will probably always struggle with some PTSD since my injury and even on good days, I have trouble being fully present in them. This is because there is a voice I'm having trouble shaking that says, "Just wait, the pain is coming."

Thus, I have to intentionally get out of my head. To do this, I crank up a badass playlist that I used to listen to while training for my triathlons or before a speaking engagement and imagine that's what I'm doing. I am training, I'm preparing for my next big thing, and it's epic! I think of what made me a good swimmer in my competition days. I wasn't the fastest swimmer, but my gift was that I could make my mindset completely present to the race. I couldn't think of how I looked in my swimsuit or how my parents were watching or what other competitors were doing. I couldn't think about the homework I had waiting for me or the test that was on Friday. To win, I had to mentally stay in the race, looking at the lane ahead of me, one stroke at a time.

The same goes with my life. I can't project my past onto my present and my future. I have to see life in each precious moment as it comes, and need to let go of the voices that tell me that my worst days are a prophecy over my life. That is bullshit.

In combating my PTSD, I've spent a lot of time reflecting on what I've learned from diamonds. I loved working with diamonds and am amazed by their beauty, of course, but even more impressed with how they came to be in our world. A diamond is just a piece of unremarkable carbon that develops under enormous force. The strength and brilliance of a diamond are forged by pressure, time, and heat. Many diamonds even come from the intense heat given off from a volcanic explosion. The past of a diamond is violent, but we rarely think of that as we wear them. The pain of the past does not dictate the future position the diamond will take in its life. As the diamond is being forged in the fire, how does it hang onto the hope that one day it will be used as an expression of unconditional love?

Similarly, why didn't I view my own suffering as the catapult before I am thrown into brilliance? If a piece of freaking carbon can have such meaning, surely I could too, no matter what my mind was telling me. I'm working on letting go of the narrative that people won't want a broken human in their lives, and instead believing that they can see glimpses of the diamond I am becoming through this.

A Cure I Didn't See Coming

My recovery was trudging along in Iowa at what felt like a glacial pace to me, and the pain was still consistently bothering me. I was extremely grateful for my mom's care and companionship, but I was beginning to miss my life in Austin and my friends who I hadn't seen in months. Loneliness was triggering the resurface of old wounds. I feared dying alone, never finding a life partner, that great love I desired to find.

As these thoughts took flight, I yearned for my dog Bridges who had passed away a year before my back incident. Bridges was a beautiful English Springer Spaniel Rescue with the sweetest temperament, and we were inseparable. There'd been a hole in my life since his passing and I knew I should do something about that. I needed a reason to get up each day, to keep trying to get better without excuses. I needed another dog.

I went onto the same English Springer Spaniel rescue site where I had found Bridges years ago. I searched the site for months until one evening, as I was unwinding for the night sitting in my recliner next to my mom, a gorgeous dog caught my eye, and I knew I found the perfect match.

"Mom, I think I found the one!" I yelped.

"Which one?" Mom inquired.

"This girl loves greeting her people with her giant smile and a desire to play. She loves walks, hikes, swimming, and showering people with love. She's a great cuddler and is looking for a forever home where she can be loved and pampered."

"Sounds like the right fit."

"What's her name?"

"I didn't even check." But then I do. "Oh my God."

"What? What is it?"

"Her name is Gemma." Saint Gemma. Miracles do exist.

Gemma was located in Dallas, which would make her easy to pick up as I needed to go back home to Austin soon anyway. This was meant to be, so I immediately contacted the adoption coordinator and pleaded my case for Gemma, even sending over copies of my vet records for Bridges proving I was a responsible English Springer Spaniel dog owner.

A few weeks later, I was overcome by joy as I answered a call from the adoption coordinator jubilantly exclaiming,

126

"Pat, you're approved. Gemma is yours!" I was ecstatic, and we set my pickup date for Gemma one month from now.

Unfortunately, that next month threw a storm into not only my own life, but the entire world. It was March of 2020, and a virus called COVID-19 was on the rise, and had entered the U.S. Our country was asked to lock down, slow the spread, and wait until we had more information. Grocery stores were flocked and vanquished. Items like toilet paper, hand sanitizer, and Lysol spray were nearly wiped out. If you landed one of those, it was like finding a pearl in an oyster. Luckily, we were stocked on toilet paper, but I made sure to buy my mom and I enough peanut butter, our favorite snack of choice, to last us months.

If I thought I'd been lonely before, now I'd be joining the globe in a loneliness epidemic. It's interesting how we can sometimes feel better knowing others are also suffering. For me, I've realized I am eager to seek a fellow suffering compatriot. I want someone who understands so that I don't feel as alone. Part of the lie of loneliness is that no one understands what you are going through. Because of this thought, we can have a tendency to stay with the comfortable parts of loneliness. At least we know what to expect. If we don't put ourselves out there, we don't risk the chance of being disappointed. When you are doing everything you can to simply walk to the mailbox and back, another blow of disappointment can feel like too much.

I will say the feeling of comfort when I find a fellow sufferer doesn't last long. I feel so terrible for their suffering, and deeply wish it could be taken from them. The saying is "Misery loves company," but I think it should be "Misery needs company to love it and show it there's still hope."

I realized if I could've prevented the world from this

pandemic by just suffering alone in my isolation longer then I would've taken that up. Instead, I soon saw so many others around the world experiencing a suffering far worse than I. I could never imagine a loved one being snatched up so quickly by a disease and not being able to be in the hospital to say goodbye. On the reverse, I also can't imagine the depth of loneliness one must feel dying alone.

With the world upside down and with no sure end in sight, I knew I couldn't leave my mom alone. I emailed the adoption coordinator that I would not be able to get Gemma on our established date, and asked if they would hold her for me until this COVID thing died down.

Understandably, she told me they couldn't hold her. They had a family who was ready to adopt her now if I wasn't able to. As much as it broke my heart, I knew I needed to hand over Gemma. She deserved a loving family immediately. She shouldn't have to put her life on hold for me.

That hurt. I thought all the stars had aligned for Gemma to be mine. It was perfect. What was the Universe doing by putting this obstacle in our path? I had no idea, but I did know that I really had no choice but to put my dog search on hold. With all the uncertainty of the world, I had no clear vision of when I would be able to travel to pick up a dog again.

Four months passed and it seemed like COVID wasn't going anywhere. However, my mom and I had established a rhythm that was working, and I knew she was set up for whenever I wanted to return to Austin. As I began to realize this, I took out my computer once more and renewed my dog search. With few safe options but to stay home, this was the ideal time to bring a new pet into my life.

A few weeks later, I found another stunningly perfect dog for me named Lindsey. She was gorgeous, loved people, and was an award-winning show dog. And she was located in Houston. I could easily get her from Austin. I submitted my application and was approved within days. This time I wasn't going to wait. I let them know I could pick her up the following week, jumped in my car, and drove back home to Texas from Des Moines.

Lindsey behaved fine in the car while on the three-hour drive from Houston to Austin, but I couldn't help but notice she was not happy to be at home with me. She kept her distance from me and barely wagged her tail. I knew she must be scared. She'd been with her foster family for seven months, which was a significant amount of time, and she was attached to them. She looked at me sullenly as I fed her.

"Don't worry, Lindsey. I know you're scared, but I'll make you happy. I'll do whatever it takes to make you happy."

And boy did I try over the next couple of days. We went for walks, swims, and hikes. I picked up special food and toys for her. I told her she was loved and sat next to her petting her and scratching behind her ears. But even with all of my best intentions, her attitude wouldn't budge. She did not want to be here. Which is when I got a call from the mom of her foster family.

"Hi, Pat. I'm really sorry to do this, but I'm calling because we underestimated just how attached our family is to Lindsey. We thought we could part with her, but the kids miss her desperately, and so do I. I'm sorry, but we really want her back. Would you be willing to give her back to us?"

As much as I didn't want to lose another precious dog, I knew it was the right thing to give Lindsey back to her foster family. Their connection was too strong for me to feel right disrupting it. So that's what I did. I drove Lindsey back to Houston, and I cried for the next few days.

When you face obstacle after obstacle, it almost doesn't matter the size of the next one. It's huge because it's stacked on top of all the other trials. I was desperate for a victory, and thus a second loss felt colossal. I thought it was going to crush me. I had felt so encouraged by all the signs pointing me to another dog, nudging me that I was on the right path, and to be let down multiple times felt cruel.

I decided that was it. I guess I wasn't meant to have a dog, and all these trials were just proof of that. Maybe I was too damaged or maybe now was just not the right time. Whatever it was, I told all my friends and family that I was *done* looking for a dog right now.

One morning as I bathed in a self-pitying state wondering why God kept teasing me with a dog only to take her away from me for the second time, I noticed my phone light up. As I reached for it, I saw that I had dozens of texts, Facebook messages, and missed calls. They were all notifying me of the same thing: There was this dog posted on a local neighborhood Facebook group that I had to see.

My friend Veronica, who is truly more like a sister to me, was a foster volunteer for another dog adoption organization in Austin called Addicus Legacy Dog Rescue. Their Facebook page had just posted an English Springer Spaniel named Nelson who needed to be adopted immediately. Nelson's foster family had a woman who was in her eighties and on blood thinners and this dog had a habit of jumping on people, and she was getting all scratched up, which she couldn't allow to happen anymore. Nelson had such a happy look on his face in the picture they posted, and my gut told me to go ahead and try one more time. I was relieved to know I wasn't immune to hope.

I filled out the paperwork immediately, and then called the head of the organization, advocating how much I wanted Nelson.

"I have about 100 applicants, and you're one of the last ones," she said to me.

"I understand, but I want to go visit him."

"That should be fine."

Turns out the foster family only lived two blocks from me, so I organized a time to stop by the next day. As I walked into their backyard there were eight rescue dogs playing. My eyes immediately narrowed in on Nelson. On either side of him were two huge German Shepherds, each one chewing on one of Nelson's floppy chocolate brown ears. Nelson made eye contact with me, and the look seemed to plead, "Please get me outta here. *Please.*"

I walked over to him, and as I bent down to pet him, he put his white, furry paw up toward me. I grabbed ahold of his paw, and in that instant, he squeezed my hand. I couldn't believe it! It was unlike any experience I'd had meeting a dog, and this time I really knew. This was the dog meant for me. The foster family came over to see how things were going when I asked, "Would you mind if I stopped by tomorrow, and took Nelson out for a few hours?"

"Well, I don't see why not," the eighty-year-old woman uttered.

The next day was a beautiful, sunny Sunday, and when I came to pick up Nelson, he jumped into my car excitedly. He was ready for an adventure! We headed straight to Lake

Travis and went for a swim. Then we headed to my neighborhood, went for a walk, and played fetch. Both of us tuckered out, we went back to my house and watched a cowboy movie together. He cuddled up right next to me, and laid his head on my lap as we were transported to the wild west, his ears perking up whenever he saw horses on the screen.

The foster family called me at five p.m. wondering when I was bringing Nelson back home as they were planning to head out to dinner soon. I knew that was my cue to end our glorious day, but before heading out the door, I turned to him and asked, "Are you comfortable here? Do you want to stay here with me?"

His eyes looked straight into mine, his tail wagging faster than ever, and his mouth turning up into a full-on grin. I couldn't help but laugh. Yes, this was a mutual love. We both wanted to belong to each other.

As I dropped him off, I told the family, "This dog is my dog and he really liked hanging out with me. We did so many fun things that we both love to do and will do almost every day if he's mine."

"Look, it's not up to us to make the decision, but out of these 100 people who are interested in him, you are the only one who came to visit, and you were the only one who wanted to take him for a day. No one else has asked to do that. So as far as we're concerned, he's yours," the older woman responded.

That felt encouraging and was good to know. I completed the remaining paperwork and sent pleas to the organization stating how well Nelson and I bonded. Veronica called the head of Addicus and told her I was an amazing dog owner. The foster family let them know they were impressed at my initiative to spend time with him. I waited on pins and needles, doing my best to keep faith. A few days, which felt like years, later Addicus informed me that Nelson was mine. *Yes! Yes! Yes! Hallelujah!* I picked him up on a Tuesday, and as soon as he was in my arms, I cried. This was what I'd been waiting for.

There was just one issue. He did not look like a Nelson. He had only been known as Nelson for a few weeks. Nelson was his given name because the rescue group names the dogs by going through a rotation of the alphabet and when this dog got to them, they were in the N's. As I looked at him though, I knew the name that was rightfully his.

"Finn!" I called out to him as soon as we arrived at my house after signing all the paperwork. His ears immediately perked up and it looked like he had a big, sheepish grin on his face. *Finn.* Yes. He was most definitely a Finn. I always loved the name Finnigan. It is a good, strong Irish name and Finnigan was my great grandparents' last name, so it seemed like a perfect fit. Thus, became his official name of Finnigan, but Finn, for short.

Finn and I began our beautiful life together in August of 2020. He loves my mom, is sweet, sensitive, alert to my moods, and always eager to play. Finn has the deepest brown eyes, and when they are pointed toward me, I feel overwhelming love. Finn makes me feel like I'm the only human in the world, and I can count on one hand the number of nights I've been away from him. We are tied at the hip, but honestly it feels more like a uniting of hearts. We just get each other. And we still love to watch cowboy movies together.

We eat meals together, but before we do, I always say a little prayer for us. Finn bows his head and then waits until I say "Amen" before he digs into his food bowl. Our meal prayers are mostly filled with admissions of gratitude, reminders that miracles do happen, even when they appear different than expected, and that God's got us, even when we don't know it.

We humans face countless disappointments in our lifetimes. Sometimes those disappointments can wreck us, but sometimes they are actually there as guides. When you persevere through the hardship, you have the opportunity to experience a victory that feels *just* right, and often even more right than the original plan. My search for a new dog was bumpy, but ultimately led me to my sweet Finn, and I wouldn't trade that pup for anything, not even to be saved from the mishaps that came before him. I've learned that sometimes a "no" is actually preparing you for the right "yes," and something in that hopeful statement makes me feel less lonely. In the moments I forget that fact, Finn comes up to me with his silly grin, places his head on my lap, and reminds me all over again. In the remembrance I am not alone.

Hope Nugget: Even when suffering, humans are not too much to be loved. Don't lose faith that a *no* could be preparing you for the right *yes*.

Chapter 11

Show Up

"Sometimes the bravest and most important thing you can do is just show up."
—Brene Brown

I have a genuine love for the holiday movie *Polar Express*. I had seen it a few times but was profoundly affected by the film when I saw it over the holidays while staying with my mom in Iowa before my first Big Kahuna surgery. My nephews were at the house, and we hunkered down to watch our favorite Christmas movie.

The story focuses on a young boy who no longer believes in Santa Claus and the magic of Christmas. A mysterious stream train arrives on his street with a conductor inviting him on a journey. It's Christmas Eve and the boy has lost hope, reluctant to get on the train. He asks the conductor, "Where's the train going?" That's when the conductor (played by Tom Hanks) says, "One thing about trains: It doesn't matter where they're goin'. What matters is deciding to get on."

I had spent months waiting for my upcoming surgery and was worried about the trials and tribulations I knew I'd soon be facing. I had spent a lot of time doing nothing, in too much agony to do much but lie face down and try to distract myself from the unending back spasms and nerve pain.

When I heard that line, I was filled with peace and felt permission to just show up. I didn't need to know where my train was going. What was more important was to take that leap of faith and get on with the journey even if I couldn't see the finish line. Like the little boy in the movie, I was distraught and unsure what I believed, but found hope in taking the first tentative steps toward recovery.

The train conductor's message reminded me of one of my favorite quotes, "A journey of a thousand miles begins with a single step." I always loved the message that even the most arduous of endeavors has a beginning point. For me, that was deciding to take that first brave step into the unknown as I walked myself to surgery at the Mayo Clinic on that freezing January morning.

We don't know how strong we are until we get tested. After recovering in Mom's tender care from my second fusion, I was now back to my life in Austin and found I needed new inspiration to continue my rehab, heal my body, and get back to the life I had built. Though I felt like crap, and didn't want to do anything with anyone, I knew I had to force myself to go to physical therapy, the gym, and even the occasional happy hour.

I wanted my body to heal and to get a second chance to

live my best life. All the sports I loved gave me second chances. You get two false starts in swimming. In tennis, you get two tries to serve the ball. In baseball, you get three strikes. Thinking of these sports always fired me, Let's go, Pat!

Though I wanted my body to achieve the ultimate comeback, I *needed* my soul to be given a second chance too. I needed to learn how to love myself in spite of my circumstances. As angry as I was at my body for failing, I was also consistently frustrated with the dire state of my mental health. I was experiencing depression, anxiety, and was even diagnosed with PTSD from my injuries. I kept hoping I could flip a switch and I would feel like myself again. *Come on, Pat! Snap out of this!* Of course, it wasn't so simple. Physical and emotional trauma were buried in me, and I was going to have to learn how to talk to myself with grace.

Though, I tried to hold onto this belief in the underdog and the power of second chances, I was struggling adapting back to my life in Austin. I was discouraged that I was working so hard in physical therapy, but my left leg still felt like it weighed one-hundred pounds as I had to pick it up and heft it over each stair I'd take. Every time, I felt embarrassed to see people that I knew. I would go to happy hour with friends but wasn't present or participating. I was a cloud of pain and negativity and because I didn't feel I had anything positive to say, I stayed quiet. That was such a contrast to who I had been, and I hated looking at myself from the outside and hearing an internal narrative that I was just a burden to the people I loved. I soon found myself turning down invitations from friends and neighbors because my ego didn't want them to see what bad shape I was in.

I was especially frustrated one day in my yoga class when everything in me hurt. I couldn't follow along with the rest of the class and was wondering why I should even be there. What was the point in coming? Why was I trying so hard when it seemed like I was making no progress at all? One of the teachers saw my defeated look and said, "All you have to do is just show up. I don't care if you just lay on the mat. You showed up, and that's what counts."

On most days, I probably wouldn't have been able to take that message seriously. Before my surgeries, I was of the mindset that if I wasn't showing up at my best then it wasn't worth it. On that morning, however, I let it seep in. It was the exact statement I needed to retain a dose of hope. Could simply showing up really be what counts? I decided to believe that was true. Why not? Nothing else was working.

Thus, I adopted this new mantra: *Just Show Up.* I went to yoga and would make a few moves but often just laid on my mat breathing. If I were struggling, I'd still show up to physical therapy, and we'd do a modified program. I started accepting invitations to try to get over my ego's embarrassment and took solace in sharing time with the ones I loved, even if it was a struggle, even if I needed to open up about the hardships I was experiencing. My victory became showing up and then showing up again and again.

If you wear an exercise tracker to my gym, there are screens on the walls that show the heart rate of many at the gym. It also gives points for taking different classes or visiting different parts of the gym. Before my surgery, I was "*Cheer4Pat,*" and the competitor in me loved racking up points. After my Mayo surgery, I changed my gym tracker name to "*SHOWED UP.*" The victory was being at the gym.

The win was showing up when every part of my body and soul was screaming at me to give up.

Over the next few weeks, people began to notice *SHOWED UP*. They could see my tracker in the spin class, yoga room, or treadmill. I'd hear people wondering who *SHOWED UP* was, and I kept it to myself for a while. Once I let people know that I was *SHOWED UP*, the encouragement and positive vibes were incredible. People became invested in my recovery, saying they were inspired by the fact that if I could show up as broken as I was, there was no excuse for them to sit at home on their butts watching more Netflix.

I was enjoying the external validation of my name being noticed on that screen, and I was loving being known as the type of woman who showed up no matter what. How cool was that? Being recognized as that kind of person served as a motivator to keep going again and again. Secretly though, I knew something was missing. Collecting points wasn't what would heal me, though it felt so good, and I needed moments of feeling good where I could take them. What I needed even more though was to internally accept that I was enough as I was. I didn't need to prove myself to the crowd. I needed to love myself as I was. That would be the greatest act of rebellion I could achieve, but figuring out how to do that well would be the real test.

My friend Kelly mentioned this to me when I told her this story. She wanted to make sure that the amount of points I collected wasn't how I measured my worthiness. She encouraged me to dig deep into what was taking place and what I was learning by becoming *SHOWEDUP*.

What I discovered was that my competitive side hadn't gone away. I've always been a competitor, and it's a part of my identity that I've always been proud of. That competitive spirit is what has challenged me to take risks, to work harder, and to step into unknowns with determination. Though I was collecting far fewer points at the gym than I had pre-surgery, I was actually *enjoying* making small, incremental progress. I wasn't giving up on me.

With that realization, I began slowly appreciating the smallest of victories. The power of that appreciation began protruding all facets of my life. Small progress was extraordinary. Progress that only I could see was fierce. I wanted to implement such a strategy in every part of my life. I became more committed to supporting my mom and sisters one small phone call or problem-solving session or laugh fit at a time. I was encouraged to be a reliable friend, the one you can count on to make an appearance even if I felt like shit and could only stay thirty minutes. I began looking less for perfection and focused on being present, making an effort to be a part of the world instead of alone with my thoughts and doubts.

Showing up was like finding the corner pieces of my recovery puzzle. I knew I needed to be resilient to face my difficult recuperation and get some semblance of my life back, but I wasn't sure how to do this. My ego kept throwing up roadblocks as, at first, I detested laying on my yoga mat doing nothing, or dragging my leg as I went up stair by stair. I needed to find a way to silence my inner critic, and *showing up* was the first productive step I took in developing a strategy to combat that thundering negative voice in my head. By showing up, I learned that though I wasn't sure where my train was headed, my mind was in the game.

As I trained my mind and body to never give up, a few guiding principles became prevalent in my life:

Don't Give Up

The first trick I learned was how to be in the moment and align yourself with what's right in front of you. You can't look down in defeat but should look ahead at the next step you need to take. Though it isn't easy when you're in a place of unknowns, harness a laser focus on being present in your body, mind, and soul. If you start down the rabbit hole of thinking about the future, the *what if's*, and all the things you haven't been able to do, it's easy to get discouraged. Don't get ahead of yourself and mourn the shots you haven't taken yet. That kind of thinking makes it easy to give up.

Instead, focus on the *next* right step for you and don't get ahead of yourself. Allow yourself to dig deep down and find something you didn't know you had. The switch is there, and it gets easier to keep it on as you start to rise and carry yourself. You'll get renewed determination, confidence, and the energy to dig some more if you stay in the mental game and don't give in to despair. Every day, try to find a little more mental reserve to propel you forward. It's time to celebrate small, incremental wins that will inspire you to try again the next day.

There Are No Boundaries

When you realize you have no boundaries, you can establish who you want to be in your healing. When you realize you have no boundaries in your recovery, that's freedom. A

141

freedom that no one else can control. You set the limits, and you need to be serious and free about how you want to improve. It's your recovery. Be a badass and respect your unique journey.

Find Who Motivates You

On my worst days, I would think about the friends and family that inspire me. They had no idea I was thinking of them when I laid in the hospital looking out the window, but the memories of our time together were like a soothing antidote to the pain and chaos I was facing.

I remembered joining a women's boot camp in Lakeway, Texas before my back gave out. We'd meet at a nearby park and run the steepest stairs we could find while carrying wooden rifles someone's husband had made for us to lug on our backs. I believe the instructor was a former Navy Seal, so you can imagine how hard the workouts were.

In the group, I met Missa, a woman going through cancer for the second time. She had a young family, and her prognosis was not good. Yet, here we were together with rifles thrown over our backs doing military drills in ninety-five-degree heat and eighty-percent humidity. I will never forget Missa and her determination to show up. We would run side by side, and then—even while fighting cancer—she'd pass me up. She is a hero, and I spent many hours thinking of her determination, hoping to find some for myself.

When feeling sorry for myself, I'd think of my friend Lydia who had breast cancer, a double mastectomy, and ran a marathon while going through chemo. Or my dear friend

Monica who went in for her first colonoscopy and came out with a colon cancer diagnosis, while being a Catholic school teacher and raising two boys. I focused on Veronica, who is like a sister to me and has MS, a son with special needs, and two other young sons that depend on her. She has monthly infusions that would knock down most people but don't take the wind out of her. And, of course, my mother, who always knew just what to say to motivate me. I took solace in how she shouldered the loss of my father. My parents were best friends and soulmates. After the shock of losing him, she became determined to live a rewarding life even with his absence.

Compiling a list of the heroes in my life helped inspire me to keep moving and showing up and is something I find myself needing to come back to again and again. I make a point to stay in contact with the people that believe in me and turn away from the doubters. Often, it's not what's inside of me that keeps me going—it's what's inside these heroes that kick my butt into gear.

KEEP ON BELIEVING

There will be days when you want to throw in the towel and give up on your recovery. I've had too many of those days to count. But I've learned, and am still learning, that you have to believe you will cross the finish line. Your definition of the finish line may change many times throughout your recovery, and that's to be expected. But there can be no room for doubt in your mind. You have to mentally push past the uncertainty and reservations.

Keep your head up and be willing to try, whether that's accepting an invitation to coffee or making another therapy appointment. Remember to go at a pace that's right for you and don your inner fighter to take on each daunting challenge one simple step at a time. I try not to obsess on the hard, disappointing days, but choose to have faith that tomorrow might be better. I work at not letting my injuries define who I am. I am much more than my back injury. I can't change what has happened. I was dealt a lousy hand but am still in the game and here to play. I can't be afraid of my injuries. I have to believe one day I will be whole and unbroken.

Above all, here is what I know: Grace softens the edges of past pains, highlighting the eternal. When grace is invited into your being, you are left with profound peace, hope that's unshakable, and faith that's ironclad. When you feel alone, know that's a lie. Take solace in the truth that there is something greater in your life beyond the pain and injuries.

I don't believe everything happens for a reason. If one more person tells me there's a reason this happened to me, I just may scream. I have a spinal disease—it's a physical problem. I'm not being punished. I'm not being singled out. Our bodies break, and often there is no apparent reason. I don't need the burden of believing I did this to myself, or that this suffering is happening for a reason. What I will believe though, is that it doesn't hurt to find purpose in our trials as we search for lessons and try to make sense of our world, all while trusting the process.

Meditation, inspiring podcasts, motivating books, fighting songs, and prayer can help you see the grace and look to something greater beyond your suffering. Believing in something or someone beyond yourself can give you a profound and joyful peace that no one can take away. It will remind you that, whether or not you know it, there is a team behind you.

Hope Nugget: Just show up, and you will prove to yourself that there are so many beautiful steps left on your journey.

Chapter 12

Leave Your Ego at The Door

Have you ever looked at old pictures of yourself and envied the person you saw? *I was so much fitter. I was happier then. Those were the best days of my life.*

I sure have.

Though I was determined to keep showing up, the novelty of the concept began to wean as my recovery took longer and was more difficult than I expected. I was having to come to terms with the fact that I wasn't going to be the same person I was before this happened. I wish I could say that I accepted this and geared up for a new life quickly, but the stubborn Irish lass in me does not give in so easily to change. I scrolled through old pictures of my hiking adventures, triathlons, and pain-free dock days with friends. A lie disguised as truth flitted through my mind often telling me my best days were behind me. I've always been an insanely positive person, but after multiple surgeries with very little pain relief I wondered if I had anything left to look forward to.

These dark thoughts felt foreign at first until I allowed

them to make themselves at home in my mind, and soon looking for positivity became a chore more than a personality trait. As it became harder and harder to have hope, I began to realize how many of my thoughts were focused on my own ego. My ego was the enemy to me showing up, and the antagonist to my comeback.

In order to embrace the new me, I would have to leave my ego at the door.

Ugh. Easier said than done.

My ego loved the parts of my identity that are traditionally impressive, the parts that I could post on Facebook and look shiny and put together. My ego loved the feeling she got when I pushed the limits and accomplished a goal I hadn't previously. She would high-five me when I made a personal record in an event or got praise for my job or was able to be a generous friend to others.

Unfortunately, I was discovering a side of her I didn't know existed. My ego was having a full-on tantrum adjusting to my new set of circumstances. Instead of her normally optimistic cantor, she now used a loud, booming voice to tell me that I was not measuring up. My ego felt good when I was able to meet goals that she approved of, those goals that make you feel giddy and accomplished. Now my goals were sometimes things like being able to walk to the mailbox and back or showing up to yoga just to lay on the mat and breathe. My ego wasn't dancing with joy at those victories. She wasn't being stroked in the way she used to be and was having to adapt to new measuring sticks. She was showing me that egos aren't so easily adaptable and the fits that they throw are often hard to counter.

A couple years into this journey, I began seeing my ego for who she was and, to be honest, I was proud of her. She was fierce, and it was because of my ego that I had accomplished the life I did before my back gave out. However, I was going to need to teach her a lesson I was desperately trying to grasp: the power of grace. I would need to give my ego grace for the shift she was experiencing. Grace would fuel my ability to talk gently to my ego and to encourage her that she is just as worthy and valuable as she was before my injury.

Easier said than done. Sometimes she hasn't listened and when that happens, I've learned I have to leave her at the door, hoping an angel will babysit her while I give myself some distance from her critiques.

An example of this took place at my athletic club five months after one of my surgeries as I couldn't help but watch a man swimming the butterfly stroke, my stroke, in one of the pool lanes. After awkwardly staring a bit too long, my ego nudged me, "You can do that!" With this encouragement, I decided I had to try. I changed into my swimsuit, entered an open lane, and began my butterfly stroke. Unfortunately, I realized quickly that the stroke that had always come easy to me now took insane effort, and I was pretty sure I looked ridiculous—more like a floppy fish than the graceful dolphin look-alike I was going for. Even still, I kept going until my body couldn't take it anymore.

And I paid for that ego trip for a week, my body so sore that I cursed myself multiple times throughout the day. During that painful week, I called Monica and told her about my swimming and ego escapades.

She responded with something I'll never forget. "Pat, when your ego kicks in, you need to kick back. Just say a prayer to be humble, breathe, and don't let it get to you." I knew she was right. This was going to be a hard lesson, but an important one that I would need to learn over and over again.

———

Some days I've been better at that lesson than others, and I know it'll be a continual journey. Six months after arriving back in Austin, I started doing Pilates at my athletic club as part of my mission to increase my strength and flexibility. Pilates is an amazing total body workout designed to strengthen and tone every part of you. It is like yoga on steroids where in each movement you must engage your core while breathing in a sustained rhythm, and holding positions that make every part of you shake uncontrollably (at least for me). It is difficult but was necessary in getting my body back in shape in order to do hikes again or begin playing pickleball.

The Pilates class used a reformer machine and when I would grab hold of the handle of the machine's resistance bands, it always reminded me of the hospital beds I spent far too much time in over the years, and the triangle handle I would use there to pull myself up out of bed.

One afternoon, I was in my Pilates class struggling to do even the modified versions of the Pilates positions. Everyone else in the class was flying through the motions, but I was struggling mentally and physically. My arms were shaking, my legs were shaking, and even my butt was shaking. At the same time my soul was shaking. Whenever I worked out, I had to combat the fear that a pain zinger could happen at any moment.

To get out of my head, I turned my attention toward the windows rather than comparing myself to the others in the class. The windows looked out over the tennis courts, the very same tennis courts I had played on every week for years. I saw people I knew, dressed all cute in their tennis skirts, walk to the courts and begin warming up with each other. I saw my old tennis partner Kim preparing for a match with her new tennis partner. I always loved playing with Kim because we both had a competitive attitude, but always made sure we were having fun too. I could see them hitting the tennis ball back and forth, and I craved the ease in which they could smack the ball, the joy that comes from playing, and the social time that forms a community of friends. I used to be them, and all I wanted was to be them again.

Somehow, I had let my ego join me in the class and as her envy increased, I began to cry right in the middle of Pilates. Luckily, due to COVID-19 and being immune compromised, I was wearing a mask that covered most of my face so unless you looked straight into my eyes, you couldn't see the tears streaming down my cheeks.

My incredible, tender hearted Pilates teacher Linzi came to check on me, asking if I was okay. Unable to answer without a sob coming out, I quickly excused myself from the class and headed straight to the bathroom. In my bathroom stall, I let it all out—the grief, the shame, the pain. After a good ten minutes, I reminded myself to slow down and breathe. I cleaned up my snotty face, headed out to the parking lot, and as I got into my car, I promised myself I would come back to another class tomorrow. Tomorrow, though, I would make sure to keep that ego waiting outside the studio.

The next day as I entered a spin class, I was determined to leave that ego at the door. I would not be so focused on my lacking, but instead would be excited and grateful that I was showing up. Immediately, I noticed a lightness in me. Instead of avoiding looking at the others in the class who were going faster and harder than me, I felt pride *for* them. Wow, I was amongst some remarkable humans, and that felt good.

I focused on each person in the room. I imagined that I wasn't the only one who had all sorts of obstacles I had to overcome in order to be here. They probably all did. Each of these humans were making a sacrifice to be here, and I was inspired by their strength and determination. My heart flowed with compassion and by secretly celebrating them, I was letting go of my need to fuel my own ego. Without that need, healing was taking place. I wasn't focused on the pressure to be better but was overwhelmed by gratitude. The ability to leave my ego at the door felt like a freaking gift from God.

Practice Acceptance

On my journey to healing, I'd often felt like Sisyphus in Greek mythology, who was cursed to roll a massive boulder up a mountain only for it to roll down every time it neared the top, repeating this action for eternity. The only way I have survived pushing that damn boulder up the hill is by practicing acceptance. Acceptance is the cornerstone of living a life of resiliency and is key in deciding that there is no other option but to move forward. Even on my darkest days, I was realizing I needed to try, try again, and then try once more.

For the first year of my injury, I was so used to thinking, "This isn't my story." I didn't want to own that this was part of my life now and kept hoping this would just be a tiny blip in the movie of my life. But the denial of the impact this was truly having on me prevented me from being all-in during my recovery. I couldn't find the courage to heal in every facet of my being until I accepted that this was real. I would have to come to terms with the fact that I wasn't going to be the same person after this. With that knowledge, I needed to allow myself to grieve the loss of my old self in order to make the space to envision a new life on the journey to healing.

I hadn't truly let myself grieve because honestly, there hadn't been time to. I was still in the process of healing from The Big Kahuna number one when the rods and screws broke, and I had to start the process all over again. My days were filled with physical therapy and trying to figure out what I would do for work and being distracted by friends, family, or Netflix in order to push aside the fear that this version of myself might be permanent.

I had no idea for sure if I was going to feel like myself ever again, but I hoped I would. I thought choosing hope meant not allowing myself to grieve all I'd lost in the past couple years, but it wasn't working.

All of us experience disappointments or have had moments where we just want to give in and give up on the life we're leading. We've all experienced times of stress, discomfort, or the shame of disappointing others. There was a day, not too long after I returned to Austin, where my pain was truly aggressive, and I laid in bed crying for hours. As the tears kept on flowing, so did the negative self-talk in my head, tempting me to not want to live. I let myself go to a dark place, one I didn't want to come out of. *How on earth do you get out of this place, Pat? How can I write a book to help others when I can't get through a day like this?*

Though such moments are heavy, I force myself to not let them win. Part of leaving your ego at the door is to accept not only that your current circumstances are part of your story, but also that you need the help of something bigger than yourself. When I become inconsolable, I've found that prayer and deep breathing are the keys to helping me see the truth of who I am. My only answer on so many days of this journey is to seek out faith because sometimes our circumstances are too crazy to understand. Believing that there is a God who loves you right where you're at, but also can see beyond your present circumstances and will carry you into the future is the core on which I keep going.

When I quiet myself and breathe in stillness, I am accepting myself in the present moment. I am not forcing my situation into my own hands and trying to fix it in this space but am open to loving myself right where I am at. Ironically, the answer that consistently comes through to my heart and mind during this quiet time is to *keep moving*. Even though I'm afraid that moving will make the pain worse, I trust the spiritual message I receive and push forward. When my pain and fear are at their worst, I focus on movement and taking that hard, first step. There is this old, animated Christmas movie, *Santa Claus Is Coming to Town* with a song called, *Put One Foot in Front of the Other*. This song has encouraged me throughout many Christmas seasons as it reminds me that I'll never know where I'm going if I don't take that first step. There is strength in getting up and moving even when you're terrified.

I remember a moment when I chose to keep moving, and

it helped me realize how huge practicing acceptance could be. It was a few weeks after I'd returned to Austin after that third back surgery, the titanium rods and screws, now replaced with cobalt. The cobalt felt foreign inside me, and I was struggling to move much more than I did with the titanium.

It was a hot Texas day with the temperature nearing one hundred degrees, and I'd decided I wanted to go for a walk in my neighborhood. A walk was proving to be a difficult task at that time, and the heat would only make it harder, but that didn't scare me. In fact, I often felt like the heat gave me extra motivation to push myself. If I could do something hard in extreme temperatures, then I could do hard things any time.

I chose to walk in a section of the Lakeway neighborhood where it was rather hilly. A half hour into my journey, I noticed a giant, daunting hill in front me. Debating what to do, I stopped under a tree for some shade and water. I knew it would be terribly difficult to get up that hill in my current state, but I hated that. It was a hill that in my former life I'd run up countless times without thinking twice. Now though, I was wondering if I could even get halfway up it. I could feel myself spiraling with self-depreciation at my lack of energy and the anxiety I was experiencing about this hill. *What am I doing? There's no way I can get up that hill. Can I even take another step? Maybe I should call Marie (my neighbor who was going through her own hell battling pancreatic cancer, but always made time to be a warrior in my life). I know she would come pick me up right now if I asked and this could all be over.*

As I reached to grab my cell phone to call Marie something snapped in me. *I am debating whether or not I can climb this hill based on my old self.* With that thought, I started wondering how New Pat could climb this hill. What if I approached this in a completely different way, accepting that New Pat would need a new strategy?

I decided to keep walking. I accepted that I did not have to go fast so I walked slowly, stopping to rest numerous times. I didn't measure my pace or stamina. Instead, I measured my ability to show up and to love myself right here in the midst of my slow, sweaty body. I accepted my circumstances, instead of fighting against them, and there was a peace inside me that I hadn't felt in a long time.

I began thinking that miracles can happen in the acceptance. Who knows what could open up for me? Already, I knew I wouldn't have decided to start this hill trek without accepting I would have to do it differently. The idea of acceptance might sound simple, but the epiphany I had while journeying up that hill led to a victory that would stick with me forever. I'd been stuck in this cycle of fighting against what my body had transformed into. I'd been warring against the muscles I'd lost and the weight I'd gained and the energy I no longer had, and the truth was, this fight had prolonged my suffering and inhibited my healing.

As I struggled to make it to the top of the hill I actually smiled. I wouldn't give up on my goal of getting back to who I wanted to be, but in that moment, I saw myself where I was at and decided I was okay with it. I was okay being this person on this day at this moment. I was okay with myself, and I could use that affirmation to get up hills, even if that meant I was practically crawling by the end. I was okay.

Resilience comes from deep inside you. It's that inner voice that you must listen to as you push the bad voices away. It means valuing your body even though it keeps you from doing so much that you love. It's the power to accept that your body will never be the same, and that's okay. It's accepting the changes that keep coming your way without giving into despair. It's letting your ego know, as Dr. Clor told me before my first surgery, "There will be good days and bad days." And if she can't handle the bad, if she can't see the slow, small moments of progress as victories, then she can wait outside the door.

Hope Nugget: Be present to who you are now, even if that means leaving your ego at the door when you need to. She'll thank you for it later.

Chapter 13

Expand Your Think Threshold

L *et Pain Be Your Guide.*
All my life, I've lived by the principle of *no pain, no gain*. It was instilled in me early as a young girl on a swim team, and further reinforced as I competed in high school and college teams. As an adult, *no pain, no gain* became my mantra as I trained for triathlons, pushed myself at tennis, or hiked and biked with my extremely competitive friends.

No pain, no gain felt like it was in my DNA, a part of my identity as an athlete. The pain of blisters, twisted ankles, or shin splints were part of the training. If it hurt, that meant you were working beyond your limits and would become stronger and faster. You played through an injury, trying to ignore the aching discomfort.

I hope coaching is more compassionate now versus when I was on competitive teams. I remember complaining about a sore shoulder and being yelled at and told to work through it by my swim coach. I soon learned not to mention any discomfort or throbbing because it would just give my coaches fuel to pick on me harder. I came to expect that competing meant playing even if I was hurt.

One of my grade school swimming coaches was a college swimmer, and he treated us the same way his coaches treated him. When I was about nine years old, I was competing in a swim meet for this coach and had been sitting on a diving board waiting for my relay race for hours. When I got up, I realized the scratchy surface of the diving board had ripped a big hole in the butt of my swimsuit. It was so embarrassing. I was always a modest girl and began crying because I was so ashamed. Luckily, my older sister, Joanne, rushed over to me and wrapped my naked bottom with a towel. At that instant though, my coach yelled, "Henneberry, you're up! Get in line."

"I have a rip in my suit. I can't swim," I pleaded.

"I don't care," he said, wagging his finger in my face. "You're swimming. You're not going to let your relay team down."

There was no turning back. Joanne told me I didn't have to swim, but I knew my coach would never forgive me if I didn't compete. Plus, he hit me right where it hurt—I couldn't let my team down.

I was swimming the butterfly stroke section of the relay, which meant that my little butt with its pink cheeks bobbed up and down the two-lane race for all to see. I could hear the spectators cheering as I swam as fast as I could, determined to get out of the pool as quickly as possible. I couldn't help but wonder if they were cheering for my swimming or my wardrobe malfunction.

I finished my leg of the race in record time, and as soon as I jumped out of the pool, Joanne was there with a towel, covering me up. She held me as I cried shame-filled tears.

The tears didn't let up even though my team won the relay, and my coach congratulated me on my fastest race yet.

I was shocked that the coach didn't care about my comfort, focusing solely on winning. I realized though that the expectation was to step up and do my best despite my discomfort. I took that lesson to heart and vowed to never complain about any physical suffering again. I learned to push through pain and injuries without expecting any special treatment if I dared raise my hand to complain.

This was the beginning of my indoctrination that pain meant progress. The message I received my whole life was simple: to get better, be faster, stronger, and improve, I had to work my body until I not just felt pain but pushed past it. I wasn't the most natural of athletes, so I used hard work as my competitive advantage. If I pushed myself to the limit and worked harder than everyone else, I had a shot at winning for my team or keeping up with my uber-athletic friends. I wholeheartedly believed the more pain I was in, the better I'd become. Pain was good. Pain was the goal.

Since my spine shifted away from my lumbar, I've come to know this was an old lesson that no longer applied to me. It's taken a team of doctors, physical therapists, and my guardian angel yoga teachers to break through my training and learn that it's time to stop and check-in with your body when you feel sharp pain or discomfort.

My new mantra became—one I hope others will adopt—let pain be your guide[1]. Pain is not something to be ignored. There are no upshots for working through injuries. Instead

---

1. *Important Note: If you are recovering from an injury or are dealing with health or physical challenges, please listen to your medical professionals on how to rehab or deal with recurring pain. For me, changing my mindset to letting pain be a guide has worked wonders, but any advice you want to take*

of working through my pain and injuries, I transitioned to looking at my recovery as *testing my threshold*. A threshold is when you've worked as hard as you can, and you're running on fumes, but you still take a few more steps down the hospital hall or swim one more lap than you did the day before.

To heal and get stronger, I had to focus on pushing myself just a little farther every day. This is different from *no pain, no gain* because I was now paying attention to when something hurt and learned to listen to what type of hurt it was. Hitting my threshold usually meant my arms and legs felt like heavy pieces of cement, but there was a part of me telling myself that I could keep moving even if it was only one more step or one minute of swimming. When I made that next step in spite of the weight of my body, I knew that was my threshold.

Working toward my threshold means I've pushed as far as I thought I could, and then I tried to perform just a bit longer or faster than the day before. That is the beauty of the threshold. I've hit the wall with what feels like no reserves left, but there's an "I can go on" moment. When I hit my threshold and my endorphins are pumping, something clicked inside—it's a mindset that I'm not going to give up.

One morning, I walked a few miles in Austin, where it was 100 degrees with 100-hundred percent humidity. I wasn't in pain, but my endurance was gone. I felt wrung out as if I couldn't walk another step but lifted my head and saw that if I went one more block it would be farther than the last walk I had gone on. With sweat pouring down every crevice,

from my experiences should be run by your medical caregivers. Everybody is different. Listen to your doctors and health practitioners.

I had my moment: "I can do this," I huffed out loud. Then I put every positive thought in my head I could muster as I allowed my mind to outwork my discomfort. Slowly, but surely, I made it. New threshold achieved! Collect 100 points!

A triathlon consists of three legs: swimming, biking, and running. With my years of competitive swimming, I'd often blow past the elite triathletes and be the first person out of the water. I'd get on the bike section and hold my own. I'd pass a few people, but no one passed me. Then as I moved to the run portion of the race, I'd watch people catch up to and pass me. In triathlons, your age is written in Sharpie on your calf. As the race continued, I'd notice the ages of people moving by me. When I was fifty and passed a thirty-year-old, that did wonders for my mindset and helped me push my threshold just a bit more. When a sixty- or seventy-year-old competitor was passing me, it hurt my ego and inspired me to try harder even if I felt my tank was empty.

One of my favorite parts of being a triathlete was that at the finish line, all the competitors would be yelling and encouraging the next racers behind them. That crowd's energy always gave me a boost to keep fighting until I crossed the finish line. Knowing there were friends waiting for me at the end kept me focused, and having strangers cheer me on pumped joy-filled adrenaline through my veins. When finding your threshold, it helps to have some cheerleaders in your corner just like in a triathlon. From my mom and sisters to my friends and neighbors, I've had people invested in my recovery and ready to celebrate the smallest of victories. I've learned that walking an extra step, lifting a new weight, or striving for another lap is easier with a crew on your side.

The recovery I was doing when I returned to Austin was

tougher than the hardest triathlon I'd ever attempted. I told myself I was training for my next race to help me simply walk a little further without pain. I began adjusting my expectations. If I can swim, it doesn't have to be ten miles when a few laps are what my body can handle that day. If I can walk three miles now and hope to get back to ten miles someday, that's great. Working toward my threshold versus fighting in pain meant finding that edge. The edge between "I can't take one more step, and I'm truly finished" to "I'm spent, but I can go a little farther or a tad faster."

What is your edge? How are you going to earn your wings, Pat? These were the questions I was asking myself daily as I faced the possibility that my threshold would be lower some days than others, and I would have to accept that as satisfactory. Finding that edge felt like a pendulum where I'd be riding the edge and feeling amazing one day, and then the next day I could barely move. Finding that edge meant accepting the days my body worked with me and forgiving myself on the days it seemed to fail. I had to keep going and remember that I had choices. I could choose to lay flat all day and do another Netflix binge, or I could get up and try just a little more activity than the day before. To find the edge, I would need to dig deep to find that inner warrior who wanted to get back to living life on her own terms.

The One-Percent Rule

How does one know they are reaching their threshold? In my case, I was living by the one-percent rule. *Try to do just one percent more than you did the day before, Pat. It's that* simple. It could be one more load of laundry or learning to walk upstairs. If I did laundry yesterday, maybe today I could try the dishes. If I walked to the mailbox yesterday, can I walk to my next-door neighbor today? By putting forth one percent more energy or focus, I could notice myself slowly building my tolerance and achieving new thresholds. I knew every day would be a one-percent victory, but even if I went backward, it was the drive to try again that mattered most.

My physical therapist and number one cheerleader, Ian, helped change my mindset about pain and recuperation. Ian was from Scotland and spoke with a beautiful Scottish accent. He was a phenomenal soccer player and triathlete, and he understood that competitive edge of athletes. He listened to my goals, and met me each week with compassion, but never pity. Even on the days where I must've had an extra irritated nerve and was in so much pain that I could barely stand and couldn't help but cry through the workouts, he never once showed me pity. He had gone through health scares before and knew what it took to get back to yourself afterward. He encouraged me with positivity and his belief that I would get through this, and we bonded instantly.

My doctors told me it would be a two-year recovery from the multi-level spinal fusion. In my mind though, if I worked harder than anyone else, I could fully heal in six months. I don't know why I chose that number, but it felt much more manageable than not being able to return to my life for two more years. Turns out, six months was a highly unrealistic number, and this belief that I could outsmart my team was not a healthy attitude, showing my hubris that I thought I'd be spared from the long recovery.

"Pat, I know two years feels like a long time, but if you

put in the work day in and day out, it's going to go by faster than you think," Ian reassured me.

For me, the *hard work* was not *working too hard*. Ian taught me to honor my body when it felt pain and to "pull back the reins" so that my recovery continued without injuring something else. This was a lesson I had to learn repeatedly because I'm stubborn, and it goes against everything I've been taught since I was a young girl. This was my challenge. I would hear Ian tell me to pull back a bit, and I'd have to fight to follow his advice. I would have to accept in my core and remind myself that a win meant showing up and *honoring* my body, not forcing her to be something she isn't right now.

Every day I would have to mentally picture myself hitting a mindset switch and owning that *pain does not equal progress*. I'd home in on the one-percent mentality, celebrating the days I could push one percent more. On those days, gratitude flew into my heart easily. On the days that my body didn't cooperate, I learned to pull back the reins. Even though I wanted to scream in frustration, I allowed my body to rest on those days. Gratitude didn't come as easily in such instances. I had to bribe her out of hiding and be grateful that at least I was learning how to listen to my body.

There are no ribbons or awards or plaques for improving my threshold. It isn't something many people see, but I aim for a one-percent improvement as much as I can. Though I used to think one percent was an insignificant measurement, I've learned the truth. One-percent victories are huge and ushered in a secret confidence that I needed to keep going.

THINK THRESHOLD

Recovery, above all, is a mental game, and I soon found that building a positive mindset was more important than any physical effort I put forth. I began to look at developing my mental game as expanding my *think threshold*. My body always used to be stronger than my mind. Now, my mind had to pick up the slack and be the conductor of my recovery. This wasn't an easy shift as all my life I'd taken my physical fitness as a measure of my success. Now I had to make the conscious shift to look for the positive even when I was feeling at my worst. I had to treat my mental game with the same energy and dedication I had once placed in the physical. Now my mind was going to get daily workouts.

I'm the most overly positive person you can meet, and even I had to admit my situation freaking sucked. I had more than my fair share of hopeless days, days where I wondered how I would rise above the storm of doctors, surgeries, physical therapists, exercise, and pain. Days where my progress was regressing, and I wondered if I should just give up entirely.

When my mind slipped in that direction, I would force myself to stop and tell my brain to get into shape! Mentally, I had to be ready to fight even if my body was working against me. I had to hope that better days (or at least a few hours) were coming. I would allow myself some time to grieve and mope and feel sorry for myself, but I measured my *think threshold* by how quickly it took me to snap out of it.

The people who were cheering were amazing, but eventually, it was up to me and me alone to muster the courage to try a little harder every day. Even on the hardest days, I tried to keep my mindset positive and focus on what I could control and let go of all the other factors that were out of my hands. Gratitude is a weapon against hopelessness, and I had to daily remind myself to be grateful for things such as my home, air conditioning, and a big jar of peanut butter. Sometimes that had to be enough, sometimes that's all I needed to push both my physical and *think threshold* further.

Focus on What's Ahead

In sports, you learn to have a short memory. You can't focus on mistakes or dwell on the lost points or the race that kicked your ass. Otherwise, you're toast. If you don't move past those hardships, then they keep on haunting you and make it hard to focus on improving your game. Athletes train to have a forward-looking mindset, always looking for the next point or new path to victory. In life, the same should be true. We need to keep that same focus on the next goal, and not just tally up all our mistakes, setbacks, and defeats.

Though I believed this advice to be true, it was tough to follow when I was in the midst of a day filled with suffering and agony. I found it useful on my hardest days to try and separate myself from the pain, almost like there were two versions of myself in the room talking about my pain and how to let it go. I imagined Pat 1 hovering above and looking down on Pat 2 who was most likely grimacing in pain. Pat 1 would tell Pat 2 that what she was going through was temporary, that the pain was not forever, and it wasn't who she was. Pat 2 would smile at this and get up, and though her pain wouldn't be gone, an outsider couldn't tell how bad it was. Pat 2 was not going to let life pass her by.

I coached myself to begin my day with fresh intention. Instead of waking up and having the first thing I think about be what is hurting, I would ask myself, *When does my new life begin?* And the answer would be: *It begins today.* Pain would not be allowed to rule my life. It might be my constant companion forever, but I cannot give it the power to control me.

I couldn't compare this version of me to the person I was before my injury. I needed to accept the person I was today and find ways to be even better, to come back stronger in mind and spirit. I knew that even if people gave up on me, I couldn't give up on myself. I would keep researching the best surgeons, keep exploring what others have been through, keep looking for the answers within the answers. *Answers give you hope*, I reminded myself often. Even if they aren't what I want to hear, answers can provide faith that better days are possible.

My fusion sister Monica taught me about the hope of having a plan. Plans are crucial in getting to the destination. Wandering around with no direction is not the solution. Thus began our thriving fusion partnership. Having been through similar experiences, we would research doctors together, share notes, and encourage each other to plan the next step, whatever that may be. If we were at a loss of what to do about our pain then we were at our worst, tempted to give up the search. Having some sort of plan made us battle ready. The plan could be to get an MRI, meet with a new doctor, undergo an exploratory diagnostic test, or to try a different yoga pose this week. We made sure to hold each other accountable to having a plan because we didn't want to be passive in our healing. We would make plans knowing that got us one step closer to hope provoking answers.

. . .

Hope Nugget: Expand your *think threshold* so that you can:

- **Be in tune with your body**
- **Push yourself to accomplish and celebrate one-percent victories**
- **Remind yourself that you aren't done yet**

Chapter 14

Why Is it So Hard to Ask for Help?

"We're all just walking each other home."
–Ram Dass

Help. It is a word I've analyzed a lot since going on this journey. Help is a beautiful word when I say, "Let me help you." It is a generous word, a heroic word, an idealistic word, and it makes me proud to say. Help is a horrific word though when I say, "I need help." It is a defeating word, a selfish word, a pathetic word, and I cringe saying it. Weird how a word can change so drastically in my brain. I know deep down that isn't right. I know it is the same word no matter which way I phrase it, and I desire to understand why I could at one moment feel great about it, and at another moment be triggered.

When I saw the trajectory of my post fusion recovery (having no idea the rods would break and I would have to do it all over again), all I could think about was the burden I would be on others. I don't want to burden people for seven months. *Aggghhhh!* So I fought being a burden. I thought I

169

could strategize this out on my own, and that once I had a sufficient plan then I could figure out the bare minimum pieces of it that would require another's help. I believed that made me some epically moral being. *Spoiler*: I was wrong. We shouldn't do that. We should allow people to help. I've learned that thinking you are above help isn't good for anyone, and waiting until you are "good" before asking will mean you'll never feel qualified for help when you most need it.

If I could leave one piece of advice with humanity, it would be, "You aren't a burden. You aren't a burden! You aren't a freaking burden!" People are living, breathing miracles. I don't know what happened to humanity that we value humans based on how much they can produce, but the truth is one's story, the lessons they're learning, and the beings they choose to love are more valuable to the universe than any measurable output from a job.

I'll be honest though, that asking for assistance has always been a foreign concept to me. I grew up in a very private family where both success and troubles were kept inside the house. If my parents bought a new car, they would immediately park it in the garage.

"Why isn't the car out front?" I'd ask.

"Don't worry. We just don't want to cause a fuss. People will see it eventually when we go to school or church," they'd humbly reply. We didn't show off, and asking people for support was frowned upon. People didn't need to know about our problems.

Like most everyone, I hated being an inconvenience to people. Before my injury, it felt so uncomfortable to ask for help and support. I'd convince myself that whatever pain or emotional trauma I was feeling wasn't that bad. I lived in a scarcity mindset, and believed I only had so many favors I could ask of others in my lifetime. I worried that if I asked for assistance with something minor, there would be no available help when I really needed help someday.

That someday had come once my spine shifted from my lumbar, and I was anxious about using up all my favors and get-out-of-jail-free cards. It was as if I was keeping score, concerned that if I asked too much of too many, I'd be left alone when shit hit the fan. I worried that people would give up on me and stop caring if I asked for comfort or solace too often. It's a shame that this is often our first impulse and one that I was still fighting against, almost four years after my first spinal incident.

While experiencing my turbulent medical adventure, I had no choice but to accept some help, and try to dampen my shame. I was surprised that so many people took pleasure in helping me in ways small and large—a text checking on me, a thinking-of-you card, hospital visit, or accompanying me on a walk around the block. I had to trust that those that wanted to help would show up and not place judgment. Asking for help didn't make me weak. It just meant I needed support to weather the storm. It meant that I knew the truth: Humans were not created to do life alone. I had to tell myself that truth often as I was learning to both battle *against* the notion that independence is the ultimate virtue, and to be grateful for each moment I accepted the fact that I need others. I would be miserable if my heart hardened so much that I shut everyone around me out for good because I couldn't get over the shame I had in asking for help.

You Get to Decide What is Helpful

In the world of the internet and social media, you can find an online group of people like you, no matter what it is. There are groups for everything. And honestly, that's a beautiful part of social media. It does try to connect us with others. Six months into my injuries and surgeries, I found groups of people who had gone or were going through a similar journey to myself. I found multiple groups for those suffering from spondylolisthesis. Spondylolisthesis is where a vertebra slips out of place onto the vertebra below it and was one of the original diagnoses I had been given. They called the groups "Spondy Support" for short, and I thought that name was fun. Many of these people also had various fusions to help their condition. I was one of them. At first, I was thrilled to find support groups for back fusions. This could help me feel less lonely! I will find my people here! I wish I had found these groups earlier!

I enjoyed sharing my experiences and tips for dealing with hospitals, long drives, and explaining your condition to loved ones. It didn't take long though, for me to develop a love-hate relationship with these groups. Everyone shares their unfiltered pain here, and it can be scary and overwhelming. People post the seemingly never-ending list of narcotics they are on, saying they are the only thing that keeps them going. People are excited about an operation one moment, and then the next they are in despair because it didn't help. You see very few victories in these groups and more and more dark spots in these groups, which I understand. When you are in your worst moment, you look for connection wherever you get it, and you want a safe space to authentically share the hell you are going through.

I remember a post from a man who was in such a bad space, saying he wanted to give up everything, that I worried if he would be alive the next day. The whole night I couldn't sleep and just prayed for this man to not take his own life because of the pain. Luckily, the next day he posted in the group that he was feeling better.

Despite the anxiety these groups were causing for me, I felt it was my duty to be a good supporter of others. Then the rods in my back broke, and as I sat in turmoil, shocked that this could be my story, I went to these groups hoping for someone to relate to my experience. I posted what had happened, and in groups with thousands of people, no one responded that they had dealt with anything similar. Suddenly, these groups made me feel even more alone. My uniqueness felt like a sentence, rather than an awe-inspiring reality. I realized logging into these groups wasn't something I should do when I was in a low place, so I opted out for the time being.

WHEN YOU ASK, BUT THE HELP DOESN'T SHOW UP

I wish I could say that once I overcame my fear of asking for help, all was good in the world but, the truth is, help doesn't always come when you want it to. One of the hardest parts of having your world turned upside down is wondering if your family and friends will not only be there but accept you for who you are now. Will they appreciate the new you? Can they help you face your bad days? Are they up for the challenge? Or do they want their old friend, sister, partner, or parent back? This is where the fear of being alone strikes the strongest.

Most of my friends are very athletic—marathon runners, cyclists, tennis players, and triathletes. My biggest fear was that they couldn't accept the person I was becoming, and thus wouldn't be there for me. I was afraid people would give up on me. I was patient with myself but, at times, wanted to give up. If *I* wanted to give up, how could I expect my friends to show up?

This recovery journey started when I was fifty-six-years-old, and I was sixty when I was compiling this book. Over those few years I cried more than I ever had in my entire life combined. At first, I couldn't talk about what was going on with me without crying. In fact, I'd have to ask myself, "How do I stop crying?" I may have even Googled this on occasion and can say there are an unlimited number of resources on this, which is both comforting, but heart-wrenching. I was sure that my emotional outbursts were scaring some of my friends and turning off some of them. I could tell from the expressions of some, that they were thinking, "When is Pat going to get over this? This isn't the Pat we know." I thought I was going to lose so many of my friends, and I did have friends who went silent on me. When that happened, I received a flood of anxiety wondering how I was going to make new friends at my age and in my condition.

I wanted to bathe in self-pity, and stalk on Facebook the friends who weren't talking to me, but I soon realized how backward that was. Instead of drowning in the fear that all my friends would leave me, I made it a practice to be grateful for the people that were showing up in my life. Rather than obsessing over the ones who weren't there, I wanted to pour into, thank, and see the friends who kept on being there for me. One particular group that kept me going was my badass yogi gals—Susan, Gwyn and Melinda. They were warriors of help on my journey. A group text that had evolved out of our yoga class became a string of messages so encouraging that I would often go back and reread the messages on the days I was struggling.

When my life changed in an instant, I was surprised by who showed up to help. I realized that some of the people that are the closest to you may be unable to deal with your pain or the new you because it hurts them as well. At the same time, the best discovery was noticing the people on the periphery of my life that suddenly came forward with so much comfort and care.

One example of this came from a young woman named Amy who was in my yoga class after my second fusion. I didn't know her very well, but she always came to class with a smile and made sure to say hello. One day she came up to me and told me she was going through a terrible divorce and that seeing me showing up to class in spite of my obstacles was inspiring. It made my week and reminded me that I was seen and known and cared for even by those I would've never guessed. Later on, she gifted me an ornament that said *Hope* on it and told me she had an identical one hanging in her house. It reminded me that hope can come from anywhere at any time.

I am sure I didn't set my friends up for success to help me because I was afraid to let them know how strong my pain was or how dire my diagnosis was. Hell, I was in denial myself, shocked at how everything was playing out. Plus, I wasn't ready to give up being that person who was "strong" and had their shit together. In the moment though, I didn't think about how I was or wasn't making this easier for my friends. I just felt hurt whenever pieces of my support system didn't show up.

I remember talking to a very close friend about my pain. She was so understanding, saying, "You shouldn't be in pain. I'll bring you some marijuana to see if that helps."

I was up for trying anything and eagerly awaited her special delivery. Guess what? It never showed. She flaked, and while I was disappointed, I wasn't surprised or even that angry. It turns out, I had other friends with connections, friends I hadn't been that close to, who ended up sending me a "care package."

When this happened, I realized how I had failed many of my friends who went through tough times in the past. I didn't know what to say. I wasn't sure if I was imposing by offering help. I might have reached out once but not followed up weeks after a family member's death or someone returning home from the hospital. I didn't have the understanding and compassion that I do now. Though the insight I have now was hard-earned, I could see it enriching my life.

We will find on our journey that some close friends may not be able to offer assistance. Our pain may be too scary or overwhelming for them. Asking for help can feel risky, but we have to push through even knowing that we may be let down and disappointed. For every close connection that wasn't there for me, I was overwhelmed with gratitude for those that did show up. For every ignored request, I'd be surprised by the support that seemed to come out of nowhere. Our family and friends can only promise to "do what they can," and knowing that makes it easier to let go of disappointments and focus on your healing journey.

How to Offer Help

I've come to dread the simple statement, "Let me know if you need anything." I used to say it myself and realize now it was often a hollow, throw-away remark. Before my injury, I didn't always have the understanding to know how to help someone in need. Now, that phrase feels like politicians that offer their platitudes of "prayers and condolences" without taking action or changing anything.

If someone you know is suffering, don't put the responsibility on them to tell you what they need. Like me, they may have trouble asking for the assistance or solace they crave. Make suggestions. Offer real actions. Give of your time. Be present. It's your actions that matter. Now, I ask for concrete suggestions on how to help. People struggling and in need often just want someone who will listen without judgment. I also keep the focus on simple things like calling a friend in trouble, sending a text, or finding the perfect card that just might put a smile on their face, if only for an instant. Side note: Ask before sending flowers. I eventually hated flowers being sent because they made me feel like I was dying.

If you are the one in need, know that the more specific you are with the help you desire, the more likely you will have that need met. For me, I've found the best comfort in being told that someday the pain will be over and that better days are on the horizon. Even if I had miles to go, being told that I would be fixed and that things would get better lifted my spirit. My sweet neighbor and second mom, Cynthia, would constantly tell me she *believed* everything would be okay. It was the best medicine.

Please note, if a friend is recovering from something, make sure you call them back, stop by to see them, or show up and offer support. Also, if friends and family aren't there for you, remember you don't know what's going on in their life. They may seem to have their life together, but you never know what's going on behind closed doors. It's hard not to take it personally, but as Ram Dass wrote, "We're all just walking each other home."

I read this as "everyone is just helping each other home." When I was down, either physically or emotionally, this quote inspired me to feel part of something larger than just my suffering. It helped me to forgive friends that didn't show up in the way I thought they would. I realized that people would disappoint you, and the strangest of people will come out of the background to help. I know now that we're all on our paths home.

My wish is that all of us humans would stop our busy life enough to look at our friends in need and be there for them. They aren't as strong as they look. We must all build up our compassion muscles and look around at who might need us. Every day we should set aside time to do that even if no one we personally know pops up in your mind. If no one in our immediate circle needs help, we can extend that thought to the needs of the larger humanity. It's a peaceful practice to have and mind-blowing how far our hearts can reach. I love that humans can feel so deeply for their brothers and sisters across the world who they've never met. It's a simple practice, setting aside time to think of others and what might be needed, but the joy that comes with it can be surprisingly huge. Though we can't physically measure this, we can feel it, and those heart changing feelings are undeniable.

Fourth Time's the Charm

I was ten months into my recovery from my second fusion, working on adapting to life back in Austin, but still in agony with a terrible sitting disability. I simply could not sit without feeling like I was strapped into a torture device, and it was impacting everything in my life. With no other choice, I went back to the doctor.

I received a new diagnosis. Apparently, I had developed ischiofemoral impingement (IFI), a rare cause of extreme hip pain. IFI meant that my femur bone was basically on top of my sit bone, pinching the soft tissue that lay between them. Now they were rubbing against each other like razor blades, and actually cutting one of my butt muscles (the quadratus femoris) in half. The medical team couldn't know for sure how I developed this, but it was most likely a ripple effect from my initial back slippage. With all that physical trauma, my body had decided to readjust itself, but unfortunately, it wasn't in my favor.

I sought out a specialist in Houston, Dr. Harris, who did a specialized CT scan that told me I was a candidate for hip replacement surgery. He encouraged me with his opinion that a hip replacement should alleviate the agony I was experiencing. The recovery process would be easier than my fusions, and I was thrilled to know there was a recommended surgeon in Austin who could perform the surgery. I had never been so happy for a surgical option.

I say the fourth time's a charm because something changed for me in this surgery. I learned to actually *ask* for help. This wasn't merely my doing but inspired by one of my good friends Zoe. She called me up a few days before the surgery and pleaded, "Look Pat, you're going to need someone there for your surgery. At least for the day." My first reaction was to tell her I would be fine and not to worry herself, but there was a part of me that knew she was right.

Zoe had recently been exposed to COVID-19 so she told me she couldn't be there, but she insisted that her wife Heidi really wanted to help me because she was wonderful in these situations and knew what to expect. She'd taken care of Zoe when she underwent a similar surgery and would be an amazing advocate for me. At her insistence, I finally gave up the fight and told Zoe, "Okay, okay. Heidi can be there for me."

I hung up the phone after that conversation and felt immense relief. I was so glad someone would be there for me and even more excited that it would be Heidi. Heidi is an amazing attorney with a level head, kind heart, and great sense of humor. Thank goodness for Zoe.

I then called my sister Carol and asked if she would be able to come to Austin and stay with me for the first part of my recovery. My family had been pestering me for weeks because I was supposed to be laid up for two weeks post-surgery, and they didn't want me to be alone. Carol said she would be happy to be there for me and booked a flight that night. Next, I called my friend Liz and asked if she would pick up Carol from the airport when she arrived. Liz said, "Of course." Due to COVID restrictions, only one person could be with a patient in the hospital at a time, so I asked my friend Lisa to drop me off at the hospital, and had Heidi meet me there after we finished all of the check-in procedures.

All in all, I had asked people to drop me off for surgery, to pick up my sister, to spend the day with me after surgery, and to drop everything to be with me for the two weeks of recovery. Zoe's perseverance in getting me to accept help is something I'll never forget. I did what I thought I couldn't do. Not only did I accept help, but I *asked* for it. My stubborn, independent self was realizing it was okay for me to ask for help and to take tangible steps in making that happen. And to be honest, it felt good.

Of course, my neighbors went above what I asked for. They organized a meal train without me knowing, and my sister and I were fed these extravagantly delicious meals for weeks. We even had to freeze half of it. This wasn't all that surprising as for years, I'd experienced the generosity of those in my circle and beyond, but this time was far more powerful. This time I didn't resist it, and by not resisting I was able to feel joy instead of guilt. Joy is everything during recovery, and I wish I hadn't pushed away so much of it throughout my life. I don't wish suffering hip pain on anyone, but I will say that this fourth surgery gave me another chance to practice what I was learning, and the gifts I received made it worth it. Asking for help isn't a crutch but a wing.

This idea cemented in my brain on a trip to Vegas for work. I was more than a year out from having hip surgery and had landed a job with a new jewelry company, who was sending me to attend North America's largest annual jewelry trade show called JCK. There would be over 1,600 vendors from around the globe exhibiting the most gorgeous gems. Even though I'd been in this industry for half my life, I knew I would always see pieces at JCK that would make my jaw drop in awe.

I'd been looking forward to this for weeks, and knew it was a big opportunity to show off my skill set for my new company. I was scheduled to meet members of my current team for the first time in person and would see many of my former colleagues who I loved!

As luck would have it, the day before I was going to leave my back gave out *bad*, honestly the worst it's been since before my surgeries. I could barely move, inching along at a glacial pace, holding onto anything I could find for support as I tried to pack. I was determined to not miss this trip, believing that if I didn't attend, I would let my company down terribly. Thus, I prayed a thousand Hail Marys, hoping I would feel better in the morning.

I didn't feel better but decided to still make the trip. I left extra early, knowing this was going to be a feat. Miraculously, I managed to park my car at the airport, get through security, and get to my seat on the plane. I felt so grateful to finally land in my seat, and marked it as a huge victory, even though my back was continuously spasming.

It was the longest flight of my life as I dreaded how my back would handle the plane's landing, and how I would somehow get off the plane, grab my luggage, and find a taxi. Another reminder that I was not the person I once was. I used to go through such things on autopilot. The pilot landed the plane fairly smoothly (thank you, Mary), but it still sent a shuddering jolt of torture through my spine. As it came time to get off the plane, I literally could not move. I was in so much pain that I could not stand up out of my seat. I was horrified both because of the suffering I was going through, and the awkward looks I was getting from the other passengers—a combination of uncomfortable, pitying, and even a few annoyed looks.

The other passengers in my row were empathetic, and flagged down a flight attendant who ordered a wheelchair for me, but when it finally came time for them to squeeze by me and be on their way, I couldn't help but feel envy. I wish I could rush off to my next event without thinking about anything else.

The airport staff helped me into a wheelchair and assisted me in grabbing my luggage and getting me to a taxi. It took everything I had to check-in to my hotel and get up to my room, but I was grateful for the help of a kind bellhop who had a giant heap of patience for me. As I collapsed on the hotel bed, I realized I would have to miss my company's dinner scheduled for that evening. There was no way I could fathom going, and my ego especially could not handle my team meeting me in person for the first time in the state I was in. As I hit send on a message to my team, I began to cry, imagining them all enjoying a delicious dinner, bonding, and having a blast, while wondering if I could measure up to the rest of them. The speculations did me no good, and I kept on crying until somehow, I magically dozed off to sleep.

The next day was the first day of the show and I was expected to work it, which thankfully took place in my hotel. I had packed my hiking poles and took them out to help support me as I navigated down the longest hallways known to man on my way to the elevator that would land me on the show floor. I did my best to put on a smile as I took turns sitting and standing behind our booth, hiding my hiking poles behind me, and never once feeling comfortable. Though I tried to hide it, everyone could tell I was in pain. Part of my job was to be able to walk around the show, networking, and checking out the trends and innovations that other companies were putting forth. Unfortunately, I was in no condition to walk around. One of my colleagues, Sherry, suggested that she go get me one of those wheelchair scooters so I could scope around.

"Absolutely not! I can't do that. The vision of me in a chair like that makes me cringe." I would not be one of those people who needed a scooter. Those were for other people, people unable to walk, and I was determined to not be one of them.

Sherry ordered one anyway (bless her), which arrived the next morning at my hotel room. I had no choice but to begrudgingly limp my way onto this scooter and began jumping through a hoop I had hoped never to come across. Truth be told, though, it was the only way I survived the show. Though my confidence weaned, my ego blushing as I wondered what others might be thinking when they saw me, I was able to do my job. I connected with people from all over the world, laughed with old friends, and gained all sorts of inspiration from the jewelry world.

As the week went on, I began telling my ego that I had to leave her in the hotel room as I went down to the show but would come back to her later. Though I was embarrassed each day, I had to embrace this reality.

On my last day at the show, my colleagues were walking back to my room with me, and one of them took a picture of me cruising down the hotel hallway, my legs straight out in front of me with a big smile on my face. It looked like I was experiencing the ultimate joy ride! I love that such a picture exists because it reminds me of how important it is to accept the help that is given. Too many people have no idea how to help someone, and it is those special souls who don't wait for you to tell them what you need, but just take action on your behalf that are proof of how beautiful humans can be. Sherry is one of those people, and her act of getting me that scooter is a memory that I'll hold onto tightly whenever I forget that there are so many willing helpers out there.

Hope Nugget: Asking for help is one of the bravest things you can do. It is an act of faith and a courageous catapult toward a community where no one has to do life alone.

Chapter 15

Be a Badass

"For though the righteous fall seven times, they rise again..."
Proverbs 24:16

Throughout the setbacks and new surgeries, friends or neighbors would run into my limping self at the grocery store, and often ask me, "Pat, how do you do it? I would have thrown in the towel by now." At first, I, too, wondered how I would manage a recovery that kept getting stalled by new diagnoses and ever-present pain. I thought, *well, what choice do I have?* But as time passed, and as I began to accept that my identity as a fighter was permanently in my cells, I was able to believe the positive affirmations others were speaking into my life. I came to respect my tenacious drive to get better no matter how many surgeries or years of rehab that meant. Now I just needed a motto that would remind me who I was.

After my second fusion, my long-time friend, Tammy, called, and as she heard the latest news about my recovery, she said, "You're such a badass, Pat." I thought about it, and something inside of me clicked. *Well, hell, yes, I am a badass.* Even though I was struggling the day she called, she recognized my strength and determination. She permitted me to be a rebel against the exterior of my circumstances and to own my "badass-ness." I felt seen and understood, and after that I began to add "badass" to the words that comprised my inner core. This would be my motto.

I looked up the official definition of badass which stated: *of formidable strength or skill* (Merriam-Webster Online Dictionary). Then I created my own definition.

Pat's Badass Definition: Someone who has faced great challenges and gained confidence and a kickass mentality. A fighter, uncompromising, someone who shows up no matter how many times they've been knocked down.

To me, being a badass meant celebrating that I was still going even after all of my difficult, soul-crushing experiences, from losing my job to losing my mobility. A badass gets on that *Polar Express* train even when they don't know where it's going, believing, against the odds, that their message and lesson will be found at the end of the train's journey. A fighter doesn't throw in the towel when their pain is at its worst but works harder to find meaning and inspiration in their struggle.

A badass doesn't have to mean that you hang off the cliff of a mountain and do daredevil stunts. It's someone that recognizes their limitations but tries to push forward a little more each day and knows to ask for help when the journey gets too rocky to brave it alone.

A renegade doesn't wait until the day they are "cured" to live life. They know there is no guarantee that life will return to normal but still carry on each day, trying to do a little more activity than the day before. A badass finds purpose and

187

drive on the road to recovery. A badass is a rebel that acknowledges their pain and anxiety but still keeps moving.

A badass recognizes the beauty in their scars. They try not to complain (I've not always been successful at this, but I try not to wallow in the muck for long). Owning your kick-ass self makes you feel powerful. It gives you that encouragement to keep going on the worst of days. Showing up day after day is a badass accomplishment. Being a fighter means that you're not looking for a big win but appreciate and celebrate the small victories.

A Badass Has Confidence

I've thought of myself and fellow people in pain as warriors that have hard-earned confidence from being beaten down by life but refusing to give up again and again. After so many uphill battles and kicks to the gut, confidence develops when you start to believe that nothing can stop you on your road to recovery.

Through these years of back surgeries and never-ending rehab, I had lost my confidence in so many areas of my life right on top of each other. My body betrayed me, I lost my job, and my social life (which was built around physical activities) vanished. I was taking hits from all sides, but I learned to honor my pain and struggles without giving in to fear and despair. Confidence is so easy to lose and so hard to get back. It takes emotional fortitude to encounter adversity or bear pain with courage.

Thus, when confidence blossoms, embrace it. Feel free to be a little cocky and strut your stuff. If, like me, you've been to hell and back, relish in your burgeoning self-confidence. Confidence gives you a little more of that adrenaline, that runner's high to get you past the trials you are facing.

I've learned though that confidence *alone* can peter out eventually. When confidence is mixed with compassion however, a boost of energy bursts forth and you unlock a strength unlike any other. A badass doesn't forget all they've been through but works to have compassion for their own suffering and increased empathy for others in pain. I believe we are at our strongest when confidence is balanced with empathy. In researching doctors and surgeons, I'd often read reviews that said, "Yeah, she's nice but overconfident." I will always want a doctor that's a bit overconfident, and if that's balanced with empathy, then that's my first pick for the team.

How Do Badasses Kick Ass?

You are a kickass by showing up. You live the fight to do one percent more every day. It means watching a Hallmark movie, crying for three hours, and then up again, researching surgeons and new treatments, or checking in with your network of friends and family. You are kicking ass when you wake up in the morning in a foul mood, and you vow to get out of that lousy headspace. You are winning when you simply show up, whether that's going to rehab or walking to the mailbox and back. As a fighter, you show up to events even when you're not feeling your best. It means keeping your head up, looking in people's eyes, and engaging with the world. Badasses go for walks even when they don't want to.

They even walk to their surgeries in the middle of winter in Minnesota—twice.

As a fighter, you have to be strong, mentally and physically. We are not in control of our pain, but we can control our mood and outlook on life. My whole world has been rehab and surgeries for the past four years. I'm a badass every day that I keep going and try to improve by just one percent more. Being a warrior is listening to your inner voice, telling you to slow down. Other times, it's following your cheerleading inner voice that urges you to try harder and swim one more lap. You are a kickass survivor when you get out of your own way. Badasses accept the sympathy they receive on their journey but are weary of feeling sorry for themselves.

One day at my dock on Lake Travis, I met a couple of my most athletic friends for a day on the water. I was attempting to get on my Waverunner, when my left leg completely gave out, evaporating every ounce of balance I had, and I fell straight into the water.

"Oh my God, Pat! Are you okay?"

"Yeah, I'm fine." I paddled back to the dock, lifted myself up, and scooched my butt back up on the landing. Once there, I asked "Can I have a do-over?"

I watched as their concerned eyes transitioned to laughing ones.

"Of course you can! Take two!"

Badasses believe in do-overs! We are allowed to hit the restart button, pivot, and get back on the horse. It doesn't matter what you call it as long as you get your butt back on the dock. There lies the victory.

HONORING YOUR BADASS-SELF

Badasses are tough. Even when faced with an unwanted detour, we get back on the train and restart our journey one step at a time. We learn that our hardest lessons give us empathy and a new toughness. Things that might have annoyed or angered you in the past may seem trivial now. You might have been shy or private about talking about good news or hardship before but honoring your badass-self means sharing the good days *and* the bad with loved ones and friends. A little badass goes a long way. It's that extra push that gets you into the other side.

Part of honoring your inner fighter is helping others to recognize the fire that burns in their hearts. You'll be even more of a badass if you help others to own their badass-ness too. Have you recognized someone's triumphs or honored their struggles? Is there someone going through tough times that could use a little push or empathy? If you ask how they are, people are willing to open up, but they need to know you'll hold their secrets and failures safely within your heart. Tell someone what an inspiration they are to you. Learn to recognize your fellow bad-asses and share how their journey motivates you.

Recently, I visited with my best friends, Veronica and Marty, and their son, Nico. They are the family I choose where we are connected by love, not by blood, but the bond is the same. Marty is my number-one cheerleader and the brother I never had. Veronica is the baby sister I always wanted and is an inspiration to me as she handles having MS and raising three sons—one with special needs. Their son, Nico, is autistic with Down syndrome, and is mostly nonverbal. As we were talking in the living room, Nico was straining to say something. We all watched him intently as we could tell there was something important stirring within him. After a few false starts, he looked at me and said plain as day, "Aunt Pat." I felt like I'd won the lottery to see him make the connection of who I was and the ability to string those two words together. Marty, Veronica, and I were speechless and in tears.

It was awe-inspiring to watch Nico struggle to connect those dots and then witness the moment that it all clicked together. That simple, "Aunt Pat," was the equivalent of doing an IRONMAN triathlon for Nico. The effort put forth to communicate made Nico a badass that day. I couldn't have felt more love or inspiration.

A Badass Cheers and Encourages Others

Kickass people keep moving forward even after a setback. They do that extra one percent more and stay with the fight even though they want to throw in the towel. I want to recognize the everyday badasses that go through life kicking ass and taking names but never get their well-earned recognition. Talented ski jumpers and ultra-marathoners are fun to watch but they don't motivate or touch my soul nearly as much as my Special Olympics swim team.

These swimmers are the biggest badasses in my life. Every day is a challenge for these warriors, but they take great pride in jumping into the pool despite their fears or worries. One of my swimmers came back to practice only four-weeks post-op from brain surgery. I am equally moved by the teammate, who has quadriplegia and is in a wheelchair and uses life jackets around his neck to stay afloat.

I've learned from this team that we are called to be a badass with others. My swimmers remind me of this every practice as they encourage one another to keep going. In competitions, I've never met a better group of people who know how to recognize and celebrate each victory. Their fight isn't for first place—badasses start the race and finish—and coming in last place is still a triumphant victory. But trust me, my swimmers know the difference between gold, silver, and bronze, and they always shoot for the gold.

I saw this same generosity of spirit years ago, while completing several Danskin Women Triathlons where finishers stayed to cheer the very last women finishing the course. Some women were just recovering from chemo or had other health issues that made crossing the finish line an extraordinary achievement. I felt such peace and community watching these women overcome their struggle to finish the race.

These final finishers had been on the hot course hours longer than many of us, and we knew their race was exponentially harder than our journey had been. I loved that there was always a fellow triathlete running next to them, encouraging them to take one more step and breathe through the pain. Being a badass is doing something hard that pushes your threshold. It has nothing to do with coming in first place or breaking a personal record. It has everything to do with completing the task and celebrating coming in last.

At one of these events, I saw a sign that has motivated and moved me ever since: *The woman that starts the race isn't the same woman that finishes the race.* I am not the same woman that walked into her home and broke her back.

Despite the pain, I am learning to like this version of me better. I am realizing that sometimes you need to be lost to find your path. I am working on a newfound badass view on everything. Nothing can faze me now. I've been through hell, took names, and came back. This is who I am now. This is who I want to be. With this mindset, my goal is to stand up in courage for myself and all my fellow underdogs in the world as we come back stronger than anyone thought possible.

Hope Nugget: You are a badass so go confidently in the direction of your badass self. The world needs that, and so do you.

Part Three

My Soul Showed Up

Chapter 16

Sailing Through It

"Suffering isn't beautiful nor is it a state of grace. But you can swim to the wreckage at the bottom and bring something back to the surface that can help others."
    —Lidia Yuknavitch

My father loved boats. He adored the water and was always drawn toward sailing and boating. When I was a kid, he smoked menthol KOOL unfiltered cigarettes and in 1972 KOOL had a special giveaway. Send in a box top from a KOOLs carton with eighty-eight dollars and you would be sent a sea snark sailboat six to eight weeks later. You were given the option of a green or blue one, and Dad picked blue. It was a Styrofoam boat with a dagger board in the middle, a rudder behind you, and one blue and white striped sail, which dawned the KOOL logo proudly. We could not wait to try that boat out when it was delivered! Multiple neighbors also got one, and so there were a bunch of what we called "cigarette boats" coloring our little Lake Halis that summer with pops of blue and green.

I was ten when we received that boat, and I would often turn the boat upside down, place it on my wagon and get it down the hill with the old transistor radio that my dad won in a sales competition. I would bring that radio and a deck of cards, get in the boat, push it away from the dock, and wait for some wind. Nobody taught me how to sail so I had no idea what I was doing, but I was a good swimmer and believed I could figure it out.

I would sit and place my cards out in a Solitaire game waiting for the wind when all of a sudden, a gust would blow forth and my cards would go flying. That was my sign it was go-time! I would direct the boat around Lake Halis (which was more like a pond with two small docks attached) and soak up all the fearlessness I felt.

Though the boat was so small that it would only fit one adult comfortably, Dad would squish us three kids in with him and would take us out, cruising around the other cigarette boats out on the water. When our cousins would come and visit, we would all wait impatiently in line on the dock to take turns for a sailing venture with Dad. There was no internet or YouTube to learn how to sail, but we picked it up by learning about the points of the wind and experimenting with how the boat moved depending on the direction it was blowing. I loved every second of it.

After I graduated from college and moved to Austin, I fell in love with Lake Travis. This beautiful reservoir in Texas covers nearly thirty square miles and reaches depths of more than a hundred feet in places. This lake was always brimming with joyful energy and became my personal oasis. I went out there every weekend I could, feeling extremely lucky whenever I was invited to jump onto somebody's boat for the day. I would watch the large sailboats out on the lake and yearn to be driving them as I reminisced on my tiny KOOL boat.

It didn't take long for me to join the Texas Sailing Club and begin official sailing lessons. I was often unsure what I was doing out on the water, and thus, became determined to learn how to be a real sailor. I kept learning, hopping onto a sailing excursion whenever I could, and even took a Bareboat Charter course in the British Virgin Islands where I became certified to sail up to a fifty-five-foot boat.

As a sailor, it is important to document every time you sail and what boat you are sailing with in order to build up a résumé so that you can qualify to captain and charter your own boat. I built up enough experience that a group of friends and I were able to charter a boat for an island-hopping sailing trip around The British Virgin Islands. None of these friends knew how to sail, but I didn't flinch knowing I was the only one. The weather was predicted to be serene, and this could be an opportunity to teach them a thing or two about sailing.

The islands were stunning and being out in the middle of the ocean was a freeing and connective experience. We laid out on the boat during the day, reading books, sunbathing, and having great conversations. Then each night we cooked delicious dinners and sipped fabulous wines. I was so proud of how far I'd come in my sailing repertoire and loved that we could have this adventure together. Life was good!

Unfortunately, toward the end of the trip, a tropical storm came out of nowhere. The day before it had been sunny and calm, but overnight the conditions changed drastically. We had checked the weather before starting our venture, and all had been predicted to be clear, but now we were surprised to find ourselves in the midst of powerful winds, rain, and concerningly large swells. We checked the radio, and there were warnings that three more tropical storms were behind this one as well as an impending hurricane. We were still two days out from arriving back at the marina where we had chartered the boat from, and we were all terrified.

This was my first time sailing in such scary conditions, but I knew what to do first. I harnessed myself to the helm, battened down the hatches, and put life jackets on each member of the crew. Then I did whatever I could to stay the course. We were beating into the wind, meaning the wind was directly in our face, overcoming the engine and sails. The eight-foot swells felt like sailing against a mountain and it took all my energy to maintain my hold on the helm.

We saw other boats from the same company we chartered ours from, and the company was dropping captains from helicopters onto their boats to get them back. We kept calling the company for help, but since I was Bareboat Charter certified, we were not the priority as they only had so many captains to go around. It didn't matter that I kept telling them I had just recently attained that certification, had never sailed in imperfect conditions before, and absolutely needed *help*!

Thankfully, my crew was great. Even without sailing experience, they were brave souls who did whatever I asked. With their encouragement and countless Hail Marys, we survived the two longest days of our lives, eventually making it back to port.

There are pubs throughout the British Islands called Pusser's and they are known for their special Pusser's rum. Once we got off the boat, we high-tailed it to Pusser's, and I couldn't wait for some rum to calm me down. I now understood why pirates drank so much. We did countless cheers to being alive over our rum drinks, recounting the story we would tell when we got home.

Of course, none of those friends ever got on another sailboat with me again.

Since then, I've been in many squalls while sailing Lake Travis. A squall often comes out of nowhere. It's a gorgeous day and you are having a blast with your crew when all of a sudden, black clouds move in rapidly and you're forced to fight against the pelting wind as you trapeze back to the marina, your mouth moving back and forth between curse words and prayers. Nothing quite humbles you like sailing in a squall. Except for maybe the personal squalls that can hit you square in the face.

In 2022, my life felt like I was navigating squall after squall, storm after storm. Realizing you have no idea when the storm will pass does a number to time. During the heart of the storm, you may feel like the storm will never end. Your mind tells you that this could be the new forever and perhaps the last thing you'll know before the end of your life.

My storm was recovery. I'd been in a series of rotations where I was recovering, my butt often stuck in a recliner, for seven months, then ten months, going on two years, going on five years. I'd been pushed away too many times from my life, my friends, my career, and my home. I'd been plagued with anxiety, depression, PTSD, fear, and self-doubt. This wasn't the stuff I wanted to talk about or that others wanted to hear. People want to hear that Pat can handle anything, that Pat is going to get back on the tennis court someday, that Pat will come back stronger because that's what Pat does. Pat always survives, she always comes through.

I wanted that to be my story, but first I was in the thick of being let down over and over again. One example was that I was finally taking steps toward my dream of playing pickleball. I had played three times and was looking forward to my fourth time with this wonderful group of people, everyone out there just having fun, trying to build this new community of friends, and enjoying an active sport. On that day, I decided to drive my golf cart to the pickleball courts as it was only about ten minutes from my house, and that way I could leave one of the limited parking spaces open for someone. When I got in the cart, I was feeling great and began rocking out to my power playlist as I drove.

I showed up, played a couple games, had a blast, and won them both with my partner. Pickleball is great because they keep switching up the teams as you go along so you never know for sure who is bringing the team down (as it very well could be me). It's awesome!

I was playing on the court during my third game when suddenly, a pain zinger radiated down my left leg. I absolutely hated these zingers as they can come out of nowhere and nearly take me out with their aggression. I'd been feeling fine. *Fine!* I was doing my thing, hitting the ball, and taking it pretty easy. I wasn't dodging after majorly difficult balls or running them down like I used to on the tennis court. My fusion sister Monica loved pickleball and she was always telling me, "Pat, the best shot is the one where you say 'good shot' to your opponent." This was her way of encouraging me to not overdo it on the court and to be wise about which shots I went after. With her words in my head, I was being very practical. I was even using an elongated pickleball racquet to give me a tiny bit more reach.

I decided to ignore the zinger. I didn't want to draw attention to it. Sadly, it was too late. People noticed. My partner at the time, Michael (this was the first time we'd ever played together), was super kind and asked me if I'd hurt my leg and needed anything.

"No, no I'm fine. Let's keep playing."

As I limped around the court, another person dramatically asked, "Oh my gosh, are you okay?"

The level of deep humility I feel as a true athlete who has a body that lets me down is excruciating. I want to challenge myself. I want to work harder than anyone. And I want to constantly improve. When you physically can't, you feel like it reflects who you are, but it's *not* really who you are, and you simply wish people could see the old you shining through. You don't want people to see the weakness. You want them to see the strength. The hard truth is, deep strength is often the kind that doesn't show off.

"Yeah, I'm fine, I'm fine," I muttered as I waited in dreaded anticipation for the next zinger to come along. I served the ball, won a couple points, and my opponents laughed, exclaiming, "See you don't need your leg anyhow!"

No one there knew what a pain zinger really meant for me. No one knew my story. I didn't want people to know my story. I didn't want to have to explain my story. I didn't want that part of my story to be retold. In real time it was exhausting to go through the story over and over again, and when I found myself in this place—once again having to stop playing something I enjoy—I wanted to pretend this wasn't my reality.

I'd gone to a couple spin classes earlier that week, and wondered, *was it the spin class? Was it something different I did in physical therapy that did this to me? Did I bend down the wrong way? What was it? I was fine just a moment ago. I was fine. Everything was fine. But now I'm hobbling on the court and can't continue.*

I looked around and saw an older woman named June who was one of the best pickleball players out there. She knew exactly how to place the ball right where she wanted it, and I admired her focus and tenacity. I never wanted to look weak in front of her, but here I was. I asked if she would take my spot, and she did so graciously.

I sat on the side of the court for a bit before picking up my things, quietly removing myself, and hopping in my golf cart to head home. I still listened to my power playlist, but my singing was just slightly above whisper level. I felt myself rapidly going down the rabbit hole of feeling worthless, hopeless, angry, depressed, and everything in between. *If I can't even play pickleball, what good is my life?*

The day before I had friends asking me, "What gets *you* out of bed, Pat? Someone else might choose to give up, but not you. What keeps you going? Yes, it is a choice, but what is *it?*"

I wasn't quite sure, honestly, but I felt pride that I kept showing up, and I knew the answer was somewhere deep in that core choice. For the most part, when I show up, I am happy I did. Unfortunately, I think that's why pickleball hurt so bad that day. I wasn't happy that I showed up. I regretted it as soon as the first pain zinger sprung. I left. I cried. I let it get to me. I felt worthless, and I think it's because I showed up and it didn't work out for me, and it made me fear the idea that nothing might work again.

When I got home, I immediately texted Monica, because she understands those days. I started thinking about how Dr. Clor said to me before any of my surgeries, "You are going to have good days and bad days." *Today is one of the bad days. How do I stop myself from going into a dark place?* I wished I had a drug, I wished I had a magic pill that would make that pain go away. But I didn't. Instead, I just had to repeat, "You're going to have good days and bad days, Pat."

With that mantra in my head, I knew what I needed to do next. I needed to know why this was still happening. I needed a diagnosis. I needed a plan. I needed to move from pitying myself to action. I had to get back to Mayo.

In July 2022, I was back at Mayo. Initially my team talked about performing a nerve ablation to reduce my pain, but after a week of tests and scans, they came to some different conclusions. Though they thought the issue was potentially in my SI joint and that I may need a SI joint-pelvic fusion in the future, they first recommended a lumbar laminectomy and discectomy. This joint surgery would create more room for my nerves, enlarging my spinal canal by removing a piece of vertebrae called the lamina, and then removing the damaged portion of a herniated disc that was pressing on and irritating the nerves around it—the cause of the intense sciatica pain I'd been experiencing in my right leg.

Basically, my nerves needed space.

When I heard that, I chuckled to myself. How many

times in my life had I just needed some space to let my irritation at something calm down?

As I met with Dr. Huddleston about this finding, he added another piece to the puzzle. "Pat, another possibility is that you could have a loose screw causing some of your pain."

"I didn't need to come all the way to Mayo to find that out, Doc!" I jokingly blurted out. "You could've called any of my friends and they would've told you I have a loose screw."

We laughed. I probably laughed a little too hard. I needed the release.

"Since we are already going in there for surgery, I think we should also remove the rods and screws from your fusion in case they are part of the problem. Your spine fused nicely and everything in there looks stable so the rods and screws aren't needed anymore."

Another major surgery.

Metal in, metal out.

As much as I wanted my comeback to be this obvious victory, as much as I wanted to be known as a badass because I got results, I was coming to terms with the fact that I would forever be *on the way* to recovery. It was becoming clear that I would have to deal with more surgeries, more questions without definite answers, more grief, more change, and who knows what else?

Over the years, while I was working on my comeback, I kept my focus on my physical and mental recovery. I could see now that there was something bigger gnawing at me. If I was going to survive groundhog's day again, I would need to check-in to the parts of me that no one else saw.

Even through these series of unfortunate events, something was taking place in me that I was trying to place my finger on—I was building confidence that I could navigate my way through no matter what may come. Whispers of motivation were telling me to still believe the best was ahead of me and that there would be new adventures to prove how brave I've become. I could sense the truth that we are all *on our way* to recovery all the time, whether that be physical, mental, emotional, or spiritual. The remarkable part of being alive and human is that we will never reach our capacity. There is always more to learn, to explore, and to discover. Though that should be encouraging, I know it can also be an overwhelming thought, one that can judge the simple daily acts of our lives as not worthy of being focused on. That's not the truth though. It is in those small, consistent practices that we develop a foundation that propels us to be able to build a life worth living. With that grace, I discovered a need to pause. In that pause, I am allowed space to process, wonder, dream, and strategize about where I go from here. What do I take with me forever?

Receiving another surgery diagnosis felt like I was in one of those squalls where the boat is leaning over, water is splashing in, and the wind is so strong, there is nothing you can do to overcome it. You just have to keep beating into the wind, beating into the wind until you get through it.

As my imagination played with that analogy, a character came to mind—me as a kid. I saw myself getting into that cigarette boat with the transistor radio, absolutely fearless. I saw myself not having a care in the world. I saw the joy of wanting to sail even though I didn't know how, and then it hit me—maybe that's the lesson. I just needed to get through the tough days, even when I may not really know how. I needed to focus less on the *how*, and focus more on the *who*, me, finding a way for my soul to keep showing up.

Hope Nugget: We are all on our way to recovery and someday we'll discover answers to questions we haven't even asked yet.

Chapter 17

Sitting in this Season

I have struggled with the fatigue of getting up every day for five years, wondering, *How am I going to feel today? Am I going to feel those shockers in my leg? Am I going to be able to sit today?* My dream is to have a day where I'm not constantly checking in with my back, where I don't let pain or fear rule me. Ever since the incident in my hallway, I've been forced to put my back at the forefront of my mind. If I want to meet a friend for dinner, I need to make sure there are tall cocktail tables so I can stand. With my job, even though I have the privilege of working remotely, I wonder if any of my team is thinking me odd during our Zoom calls for using a standing desk and never sitting down, even when our meetings last hours. They probably don't notice, but the mental preparation it takes for me to gear up physically for long meetings is an extra step I never would've considered before. And of course, even though I keep searching for ways around it, my back has forever impacted my athletic participation.

Before I would have the surgery to get the rods and

screws removed, my friend Gwen convinced me to try a Yin Yoga class with her. Yin Yoga is a slower practice that focuses on holding one position for a longer period of time than normal yoga (even up to five minutes or more per pose). Keyword: Holding. Not forcing. In my first class, the instructor demonstrated the first position we were all supposed to start with. Everyone began moving into place, but I knew it was a position my fused back wouldn't let me warp into. Instead, I used a strap to hold my foot in place so that I could hold my back while working on sitting up. Everyone else was leaning over to the side, something I could no longer do. Instead of focusing inward like I was supposed to, my eyes darted around the room. At first, I told myself this was to see if anyone else was using a modified version of the move that I could replicate, but soon it became self-loathing as the class continued and I saw every other person perfectly mold into the correct positions and then grab bolsters to help them relax even further.

I was in no shape to relax. This felt like torture as my body just wouldn't work with me to get into any sort of position that remotely looked the assigned task. I was working so hard, sweat pouring down my forehead, but I still couldn't do any of it. A few poses in, I had no choice but to just close my eyes, imagining myself anywhere but here, doing my best to simply survive. As my eyelids closed, I felt a hand on my back. With the touch, my eyes fluttered open and I realized the instructor was the one touching me. I didn't know him. This was my first time meeting him, but I could tell he was a healer. I'd seen him going to others and helping them ease into their position, and now it was my turn. As his hand touched my back, applying some firm pressure, I was guided to stretch a little more, and I did.

And then I began full-on crying.

Great. Another exercise class where I let my emotions take over. I couldn't help but think, "Oh Pat, are you so freaking hard-up to have someone touch you, that you have to cry in a Yin class when a guy you've never met puts his hands on you?"

But I knew that defensive voice wasn't at the heart of what was happening. I understood healing was taking place at the same moment I recognized the irony of this. It was in this very space, in a different yoga class, where the rods in my back broke. Gwen had been next to me then, and she was here now. Though many things had changed, some things had not. Now something else was breaking in me.

It took me awhile to process what took place in that class but as I looked up the purpose of Yin Yoga, I realized that in holding positions for an extended amount of time, you are more open to sit with the deepest parts of yourself—the hardest, most uncomfortable feelings, thoughts, and physical sensations. No wonder I was bursting into tears. I was sitting here, giving space to all that I was. I couldn't trap my emotions here. In this sacred moment, they were let loose.

As I thought about it more, picturing myself struggling to sit up tall, the instructor coming over and meeting me exactly where I was without judgment or selfish motives, I discovered how I wanted to show up for myself. I wanted to sit in the season I am in, looking at myself with love and grace, and one of my least favorite practices—patience.

Too often I was focusing on pushing myself out of my reality, waiting for things to ease up so life can be good. As Yin would show me though, sometimes the deepest lessons occur by simply holding your stance for longer than is comfortable. My physical body has been moving slower the past few years, but internally my soul never wanted to slow down. It has been working overtime rushing to get out of this state, believing if I just worked the part of me that wasn't broken, it would make up for the physical parts of me that were. I was spending so much time willing myself to enter a different season that I was forgetting to see the beauty in the one I was in.

Though I admired the determination of my spirit, I also wanted to give her the space to be present to the moment. To sit and stay and have a chance to catch up to all of this so that the lessons I am learning become rooted and not fleeting. It was time for her to sit awhile. Not forever. But a while.

Hope Nugget: You don't have to rush out of the season you are in. Sit and stay awhile so you can soak up the lessons you need.

Chapter 18

A New Kind of Gym

Setting goals has always been an exciting adventure for me. Many of my most rewarding moments have been when I met a goal I had set out months, or even years, before. It was one of those pieces of me that felt invincible. All I needed was to be intentional and work my ass off, and I would meet the desired goal.

When my body stopped cooperating in the way I wanted it to, everything shifted in me. There were so many physical goals I didn't meet. I kept hoping my body would get back to where she'd been before, but trial after trial replaced those hopes. I cursed my body time and time again. I hated her and was frustrated with her and was in disbelief that she could let me down like she had.

After five years of this struggle, coming into another recovery after this surgery to remove my rods and screws, I couldn't take the misery anymore. I knew that in order to survive, I needed to accept that my body is not the enemy. She is my friend, and though she's been through the wringer and isn't firing on all cylinders perfectly, she matters. She matters to *me*. And she is doing so much more than I've given her credit for. She fills my lungs with oxygen, she makes sure my heart is pumping blood and nutrients throughout my body, and she oversees that my brain is sending all the messages I need it to so I can have meaningful conversations with the people I love. I need my body, just as she is. I could not thank her enough for still kicking, for being a fighter, and for not abandoning me even though I've given her reason to. My body is full of forgiveness, and I must learn to follow her example. She has taught me that blame is a backward game, and hope is still embedded in my cells.

"You are not done yet," she whispers to me as she works overtime to get that message into my nervous system.

I knew mental toughness and a healthy spirituality were vitally important to living one's best life, but I don't think I ever looked at training them in the same way as my body. They are far harder to measure, and far easier to assume that they're good when you are good. Now though, I see how they are *everything*.

Why am I still here? It is the question I have to ask myself every day in order to not give up, in order to not become fixated on all the old parts of my life that are no longer present. Asking myself that question has been at times a thrilling and, honestly at other times, stagnant, way to go through my week, but it gets me through, and it lurches me out of my own self-doubt and into the ether of the rest of the world. Discovering the clues to success looked different now. It's less about the what, and more about the why.

I've realized I sweat in new ways, and though my body

plays a significant role in that, I now am learning to be guided by my heart and soul even more. Together, they remind me that I am still on this earth, and the truth of that is not for me alone so why not wake up each day with the desire to find out who it's for.

Though that all sounds positive, I can only ask myself such questions when I don't let grief define me. In this journey, I've allowed countless days where grief was pinpointing all that I've lost. My brain would list thing after thing after thing that was no longer mine until I felt paralyzed by depression. To combat letting those thoughts take over my days, I had to start looking at all I was gaining instead. When a sacrifice is made, something else blossoms in its place. Though I was losing much, I knew additions were taking place that required tallying.

I've added huge levels of gratitude for what I once thought were the smallest of things.

I've added the feeling of authentic compassion for just about every person I come across.

I've added a seat for grace at every table I am placed at.

I've added the ability to see the gifts in others and to ask them to use those gifts to help
others (myself included).

I've added increased vulnerability into my conversations and have loved the way it opens up a new depth of relationship with others.

I've added a prayer rhythm where I look at my worth through God's eyes instead of the world's.

I've added viewing being present with my family and friends as the greatest of victories.

These are the superpowers I've gained and honestly, the most important pieces of who I am. Yes, I've lost much, but

I can wholeheartedly say the gain has been more, much more.

Humans generally want to be as prepared as they can be for every situation. It is often an unrealistic desire, but many of us try to champion it anyway. I've had thoughts while training for a triathlon of what this was doing to help me as a survivalist. *What if I got lost while running or hiking one day, and it added extra miles to my route? How far could I go without stopping?* In those mental conversations, I felt an extra nudge to train just a little harder. I was going to be as prepared as my body would let me for whatever could happen. I was making sure I had everything it took to survive.

I don't think I ever thought about how my soul was preparing though. Such a thing doesn't have the same, easy measurables the gym does. I was learning though that more important than strengthening my physical muscles, is what I'm doing to strengthen my soul muscles. They require intention and conditioning just like my physical body, and I wished I realized that before all of this.

With that in mind, I decided to participate in a new type of gym that I must go to each week. It includes a game plan for training in a way that doesn't neglect the key components of survival.

A New Gym : Pat's "Training Your Soul" Boot Camp

- Make daily gratitude lists[1].
- Reach out to someone on your mind and check in on them.
- Pray every day, and maybe even join a prayer group.
- Journal (if you don't like to write, try doing voice recordings to capture and process your thoughts).
- Do research (but set a time limit so you don't spend your whole day in the black hole of the internet).
- Get out of your comfort zone by trying something new (like yoga, which I never thought I would like and now it's been key in my life and recovery).
- Speak love over your body, mind, and spirit.
- Remind yourself that you are a living, breathing miracle.
- Hug yourself, stretch, walk, get your heart rate up.
- Go outside. Breathe fresh air. Feel the sun warm your face.
- Do something purely for joy.
- Schedule fun in your week (something where you aren't focused on being productive).
- Have a morning routine that will get you up and excited. For me that's *Good Morning America*

---

1. Don't forget the little things. Examples of things on my daily list are comfy pillows, heat, ice packs, and the invention of Tylenol.

(Robin, George, Michael, and some coffee are the perfect motivation), and a phone call to Mom to see how she slept.

- Give yourself time and space to grieve, but don't get stuck there.
- Set an intention for your day—choose a word to incorporate or a task to accomplish or a goal you are making steps toward. In yoga, the teacher always asks us to start with a personal intention. It's not something I truly thought about before, but whenever they mention it in class, I'm able to come up with more than one, and it helps.
- Don't waste your day on your phone or computer. Look up and look out.
- Create a killer playlist that you can press play on whenever you get in a funk.

Some of these I did before my injury, but others I wish I'd done more to prepare my soul for getting through this unexpected season I keep finding myself in. This list isn't composed of incredibly difficult tasks, but they are often the pieces we neglect. I am guilty of making plenty of excuses to not prioritize them. Whether I thought I was too busy, or that by simply acknowledging that these things are "good" that would suffice as practice. My condition has mostly been diagnosed as a physical problem, and it makes the most sense to address it as such. However, I've realized it's so much more than that, and I'm grateful for the discoveries I keep finding on the path to staying hopeful, present, and alive.

. . .

Hope Nugget: Don't neglect doing some soul training. It's the most important work we can do.

Chapter 19

Burning the Beads

"We are afflicted in every way, but not crushed; perplexed, but not driven to despair; persecuted, but not forsaken; struck down, but not destroyed..."
2 *Corinthians* 4:8-9, *ESV*

One of the most encouraging parts of this journey has been the number of people in my life who are constantly praying for me. I believe that in many of my darkest moments, I kept going because I could feel the energy of a prayer being said about me. I could feel that someone cared enough to bring my case before God, and in that I knew God cared more than I could understand. I came to depend so heavily on this feeling that I became afraid of losing it.

There were days that I wasn't in severe pain, where I felt good and hopeful, but I almost didn't want to share this news with my prayer warriors. If I shared good news with my friends, would they feel the need to keep praying for me? Don't we as humans most often appeal to God out of desperation, and if my loved ones didn't think I was desperate, would my name flow from their lips in their fierce, daily prayers? Could I survive without prayers?

The truth is prayers don't stop working. A prayer, once prayed, does not have an expiration date. I believe it is recorded in a giant book in God's hand, and as an omniscient being, God does not forget like us humans do. All prayers are recorded and *remembered*. On top of that, prayers of praise and gratitude are equally healing. Acknowledging progress and the miracle of an answered prayer can be the ultimate encouraging force driving us forward. To know that prayers can work is the antidote to hopelessness.

I have come to wear a long strand of prayer beads as a bracelet that wraps around my wrist five times. I own a variety of colors and tend to give strands to special people in my life as a thank you for their prayers. Often people will ask me what they are, and I say "Oh they're prayer beads! But they aren't there to remind me to pray, though I do, but to remind me of all the thousands of Hail Marys I've uttered, the countless prayers that have been said for me, and all the beautiful people who have uttered those prayers." They are a beacon of knowing I am surrounded by love and that God sees me and is in the habit of answering prayers, even prayers as small as me.

A close friend of my family is Sister Jude Fitzpatrick. I call her Aunt Jude and besides being a Catholic sister, she was my grade school basketball coach and is my mom's best friend. She always says she's "burning the beads," which means she has a rosary in her hands and is saying lots of prayers for whatever topic or person needs praying for. She's often said that phrase to me as a way of assuring me that I am kept in her prayers. This phrase has caught on in my family, and our response to any request for prayer is, "I'm burning the beads."

I am part of a humanity that loves one another through prayer, and who will go in and vouch to the Universe for each other. I feel these prayers and it is knowing that others are praying for me that I see the kindest, most beautiful parts of the human spirit. We were created to care about others. We were created to do life together. And God smiles down on that. In both the days of victories and the hard moments of despair, I never want to forget how people are praying for me, and that my story is so much bigger than what I see with my own two eyes.

A group of gals I went to Benedictine College with started a Rosary group a couple years ago where once a month we meet on Zoom to say the Rosary together. We used to all live in the same dorms, and it's amazing to still be in touch and get to check in with one another about life. The leader of the group, Amy, always starts our time by asking if anyone has a special intention they want to bring forward. I usually say, "*Me!*" Then I give them the latest update for whatever surgery or therapy I am embarking on soon.

Though I am so grateful for this intentional space in my monthly calendar, I can also feel guilty for always asking for prayer. I know all the other women have their own challenges they're facing, and I am grateful I can be there for them too. Yet the journey of the past few years has led me to depend so much on this time with them.

On one of the more recent calls, I apologized for asking for prayers *again* to which I was hit in the face with a blast of amazing women basically telling me to shove it.

"Asking for prayers is what this group is for, Pat!"

"We *want* to know how to pray for you!"

"Let us be there for you!"

"Never apologize for asking for prayer! It shows that you believe in it!"

And, oh boy, do I believe in prayer. I've learned though, that my belief is doubly effective when surrounded by the uncanny abilities of fierce females to shoo away guilt in an instant.

Prayers without action is something many people critique, and I absolutely understand that. But I will say the team I have around me who are actively praying *are* doing something. I felt it and still feel it. My gratitude for each prayer warrior in my life is the fuel that keeps me going, and keeps me focused on serving others wherever I go. If you ever tell me you are praying for me, I will tell you thank you and I'll mean it from every fiber of my being.

So, *thank you* to all my prayer warriors who not only continue to pray for my healing, but for my career, my family, for each and every surgery and diagnosis, and for the state of my heart. Thank you for generating my recovery with sacred words and faith beyond what I was capable of on my own. You make the greatest team and I love each and every one of you. You are why I keep going.

Through my own practice of prayer and the prayers of the people around me, I've come to know the truth in these statements:

- Hope comes from God. Despair does not.
- If you see the moon, you will see the beauty of God.
- If you see the sun, you will see the power of God.
- If you see a mirror, you will see God's best creation. So believe it.

- Believe that God's plan is better than your own (as a planner this is extra hard for me).
- We are all tourists, and God is our travel agent who has already identified our routes, bookings, and destinations. Trust him and enjoy your life today.

Hope Nugget: Remember that we all need prayers and those prayers never expire.

Chapter 20

Search for Hope

"Where there is ruin, there is hope for a treasure."
—Rumi

H ope is often hidden, but it doesn't stay hidden out of spite. No, sometimes hope takes longer to appear because in order for hope to stick, you have to put in the work of finding her. When despair seemed the most tempting in my life, I am so grateful that I held on for one more breath, and another and another. Otherwise, I would've missed out on the signs that proved hope wasn't done with me yet, signs that signaled I was on the right path and more was ahead of me than I knew. I've shared a few stories of these hope signs, but I have one more I want to embrace on these pages.

In 2015, my dad died unexpectedly. He was only sick for a day or two, but by the time the ambulance picked him up and arrived at the hospital, he was immediately put on life support. I was living in Austin, but as soon as I got the news, I rushed home to Iowa.

When I arrived at the hospital, I could see that mom was beyond exhausted. She'd been up for over twenty-four hours and her physical and emotional being were wrecked. I told my sisters, "You take Mom home and get some rest. I'll stay with Dad tonight."

Mom didn't want to leave, but we persuaded her to go, and as she left the room, she told my dad not to go anywhere, and that she would be right back. Once they were gone, my focus shifted from my mom onto the reality of what was happening. My dad was leaving us, but for now it was just me and him, all alone in this hospital room. I looked down at him, the man with a fierce spirit, who spent his whole life working harder than I'd ever seen anyone to make sure his family knew they were loved and cared for. Even in this vulnerable state, there was strength flowing through him. I felt it as I grabbed his hand and held onto it. I sat with him, allowing the rhythm of the medical machines to soothe me as I tried to gather my thoughts and emotions. I knew it would be a while before my family returned as they had only been gone a few minutes, but I didn't want to waste whatever alone time I had left with dad. There was so much I wanted to say, and yet I knew what my dad would be most worried about at this moment. I decided to address that first and whispered, "Dad, don't worry. I'll take care of Mom." At this my dad squeezed my hand, let go, and the rhythmic beeping escalated into an orchestra of buzzers and alarms all going off simultaneously.

Nurses came rushing in, and before I could get a word out, one yelled, "He has a do-not-resuscitate order! He's gone."

My mom had only been gone for five minutes. She would be devastated that she wasn't here. I wanted to scream, but instead a squeaked out version of, "But my mom needs to say bye to him," was all that came out.

The head nurse put her hand on my back and uttered, "No. He chose to leave when your mom was gone. He decided when he wanted to go."

"No, no, no! Can we fake his death so my mom is here? Can I get her back and we fake it so she thinks she was here for this moment?" I was desperate, but the nurses urged me against this plan.

They had told me that on life support, hearing is the last sense to go. I wondered if dad heard my message and that's what gave him the peace to pass on. It turns out my mom had just pulled out of the hospital parking lot when he left this world.

I immediately called my sisters and told them to get back here right away with mom. I didn't tell them why, but just that they needed to come pronto. They had barely left and were back within minutes. Nothing wrecked me more than seeing them all register that dad was gone.

At my parents' home the next day, my mom was a rock, but at night, once her bedroom door was closed, my sisters and I could hear her crying for hours. My parents were the strongest love match I'd ever seen, and the grief at his passing was heart-wrenching.

A few days later, everyone was out of the house, and I was home alone. I was cleaning up and vacuuming, standing at the bottom of our basement stairs right under a smoke detector. As I vacuumed, it started chirping, signaling it needed a new battery. I could only find one battery in the house so when Mom came back from the store, I told her, "We need to change all the batteries in the smoke detectors because one went off right above my head while you were gone."

"That doesn't make sense. Dad and I replaced all the batteries a few weeks ago." That's when I knew it was a sign from my dad. This was his way of telling me it was all going to be okay.

A similar incident occurred a few days after my initial injury took place in 2018. A few friends and neighbors were over, hoping to provide some solace in my suffering. I couldn't move and was lying face down on my bed with my face leaning over the edge of the bed. My friend Liz, one of the sweetest, funniest humans I know, lay down on the floor right under where my head was so that we could be face to face. If that wasn't enough, she spent her time there telling jokes and trying to make me laugh.

Everyone was surrounding me, assuring me it would be all right, but I had so much pain and had too few answers. I was beyond consoling (aside from a chuckle or two at one of Liz's jokes). Other than my dad's passing, I was at the lowest point in my life. I had not only lost hope, I'd forgotten it even existed.

Then my smoke detector started chirping. My house has a main room with a very high ceiling and, of course, that's where the annoying chirp-chirp-chirp sound was coming from. Suddenly, I was awash with peace and knew it was a signal from my dad. Just like with what happened in Iowa, I had replaced the batteries a week prior. As my neighbors brought in a super tall ladder and replaced the battery, I had the same feeling of being watched and protected as I had three years earlier when my dad first passed and the smoke detector had blared right above my head. Feeling my dad's loving presence, I had a glimmer of hope again. It felt like both a strong hug and a gentle nudge to remember I wasn't alone and that there was room for optimism.

One could say that the smoke detector story was just a coincidence, but deep in my gut I knew it was something more. It became one of those pivoting moments where I vowed to always be open to hope. Whenever I have hard days, days where I don't think I can keep going, hope leaves me clues that I am loved and that there is a version of me on the other side of this that is worth fighting for. Hope has become my consistent comforter and my foundation for resiliency.

What Does it Feel Like to Have Hope Back?

When I have hope, I feel like I can take on the world. My pain might still be high, but with hopefulness on my side, I can banish—if only for a moment—the lies that anxiety and fear have been trying to sell me. With hope, there is a vision of a future where my back pain is manageable, and I can make plans for a new life. Instead of waking up with no blueprint at all, hope lets me dream of better days ahead. The steady stream of questions bouncing around in my mind is replaced with grace. When I have hope, it's like riding the easiest wave to shore. And like the ocean waves, hope ebbs and flows within me.

I've learned how fragile hope can be and how it needs to be nurtured to fight against the dark forces of fear. When you are filled with it, you want to hold on forever and savor every moment. Optimism can be fleeting, and sometimes if you try and grab it harder, it slips through your fingers. Thus, hope teaches us to live in the moment, not knowing when its warmth will shine again but ready to enjoy every moment of its healing powers.

Hope often takes me by surprise. I can be having the worst day of physical pain when its vice grip eases ever so slightly. Suddenly, I'm able to take a deep breath or two, not even aware that I had been holding my breath to grit through the pain. My first thought is gratitude, but then it is often followed by "How long will this last?" I have to remind myself to stay present and not question how hope arrived or how soon it might go away.

Hope frees me to make plans, even if it's just a plan for that hour. Having a plan makes all the difference in the world. It's something to fight for and a distraction from fear and anxiety.

Hope comes in many forms. There's the relief when your doctor says, "We'll figure this out." There's excitement when you have the energy to tackle a project. There's peace when you are able to laugh fully at one of your ninety-year-old mother's jokes. Ultimately, hope is a catapult.

Moving from Despair to Determination

What I didn't know before my injury is that having hope is a choice. Even in the most trying of times, we can choose hope over despair and optimism over sorrow. It's a mindset shift that even in our most hopeless moments, we still have control. I can't magically fix my back or make the pain stop, but I can focus on the promise of better times. I can hold tight to the dream of being physically healed and emotionally restored.

It's a magical feeling to move from despair to determination, to realize that not every day will suck, and for that brief insight, a new life seems possible. It's a huge relief, even if it's just for a few moments. When I wake in the morning and lay there with no pain, no words can describe how monumental and invincible I feel. I know it won't last, but I relish those few minutes of peace. I don't want to move. I lay there and remember how it feels to have no pain. It makes me clear, appreciative, and helps me the next time pain takes over and attempts to decrease the hope I've built up.

If your recovery gets derailed as mine did with another surgery (and another and another), you have to have a plan on how to find hope on your own. Hope is the antidote to fear and loneliness, and when you have it, even on your worst days, you can see beyond your suffering.

Hope isn't always right in front of your face. You have to seek it out and create opportunities for hope to inspire and enrich your life. This means keeping your head up and ears open for signs that inspire and move you to continue healing. For me, hope tends to smack me in the face in the form of others.

I've found hope looking into the eyes of my rescue dog, Finn. I've found hope in the hallways of Mayo, seeing countless individuals praying for answers and putting their faith in compassionate doctors. I've found hope in writing out my story. I've learned so much in this journey of finding my voice, and to share those lessons gives me hope that there is much more to do and to be.

I've found infinite hope in watching my Special Olympics team, *Thunder*, swimming back and forth in training. I'm inspired to see their progress from season to season. It's humbling to watch some of my swimmers with severe anxiety issues persevere even though all the races and crowd noise is hard for them to bear. I gain such strength seeing my swimmers jump into the cold pool water. For most people, there's the initial shock as they hit the water, but for my swimmers, jumping in the pool is a sensory overload. They hate it, but they still come back to practice over and over again.

One swimmer in particular who has continually inspired me is a young man named Travis. He has high anxiety so loud noises, cold water, and anyone touching him bothers him. He is a good swimmer though, so it became our plan to find ways to help with the noises and touching. That's a difficult task in the echo chamber that is an indoor pool, especially during a meet where coaches, family, and teammates are constantly cheering.

Our coaching strategy became patience. Us volunteer coaches as well as the swimmers' parents were committed to not forcing any of our swimmers, including Travis, to jump in the pool if they weren't ready. We did not pressure or manipulate. Instead, we encouraged that this was a safe environment and we let the swimmers become a community, a team. We noticed that the swimmers learned the most from one another, gaining courage from the actions of their teammates.

At the beginning of the season, Travis was hesitant to get in the water and once he did, he was swimming with great difficulty. I could see the potential in him, but he was having trouble trusting his body in the water. He kept using more energy than was necessary and constantly lifted his head out of the water instead of getting into a rhythm where he could feel his body balance in the water. I hated to see how hard it was for him, but I was in awe of how he always showed up. Even when frustrated, he came and participated.

I knew there was no way to rush trust, and thus, was floored to see that after a few months trust was creeping in for Travis. He actually began to relax in the water and ease into his stroke. By the time the season was ending and we were headed to the big state swim meet in College Station, Texas he had one of the best strokes on our team.

The state meet took place at Texas A&M University where the swimming facilities were breathtaking. As we took in their gorgeous, Olympic-sized pool, we couldn't help but feel inspired. The whole Thunder team was in the midst of a moment they worked so hard for.

We had a fun and successful time as many of our swimmers had placed and were adorned with medals. After day one, we had a celebratory dinner with the swimmers and their families at a crowded, but delicious Italian restaurant. As I looked around, I was overwhelmed by the joy exuding from my swimmers, including Travis, who was laughing with friends and downing some pasta. Travis's dad came up to me during that meal and said, "Travis never would've done this a year ago. He never would've come to a crowded restaurant with a bunch of people and sat with friends laughing like he is."

My eyes teared up at this, and it's a moment I come back to in my memory whenever I'm looking for hope. Travis became one of our best swimmers and is an incredible human. He is an amazing example of what I see week after week when all these swimmers decide to show up to practice even though at times it's excruciating for them. They are all so special and I could tell countless stories of the amazing feats they've accomplished as well as their parents. The Lake Travis Thunder Swim Team is a beautiful mosaic of humans who all stay committed to trying their hardest to grow through love, patience, and encouragement. They are the embodiment of hope.

Hope Nugget: Don't let despair win but go on a search for hope every day. It's often right under your nose if you allow yourself to see it.

Chapter 21

Practice Compassion & Empathy

W hen I first learned I'd have to have a second spinal fusion surgery and start my recovery over, I was angry. I was so irritated that I became impatient with those I loved as well as myself. I lost my temper more times than I want to admit, snapping at people and cutting off conversations because I didn't want to talk about my surgeries or new recovery. The anger stemmed from my disappointment that I'd done everything by the book, and still had to go through it all again. I felt like a horse had kicked me in the gut, forcing me backward onto a path I had already walked. I felt like I was being punished and I didn't know if I had the strength to start all over again. This cocktail of emotions made me pissed off at the world and practically everyone in it.

It was easier to release my anger than to give in to the fear and grief at the root of my distress. I thought if I allowed myself to feel the anxiety and sadness, I would go so deep there'd be no way to come back. But anger has a way of putting everything on hold.

It took me a few months to realize that the anger inside

of me was helping no one. It didn't make my pain go away. It didn't magically fix my spine. It just made me doubt my purpose in life and acted as a chasm pulling me away from those closest to me.

I realized I needed a reboot. I needed to power down and refocus on what really mattered to me. Almost everything that stops working will start again if you unplug it for a few minutes—including you. It's funny how most of the time, that works.

As I sat quietly, trying to regain my fire to fight, I reflected on the gifts I had received on my path to recovery. I acknowledged my anger but vowed to no longer let it rule my days. I saw that my painful journey had changed me for the better. Did I wish I could have learned these lessons without multiple back surgeries? Of course, but I'm stubborn and hard-headed at times and maybe this was the vessel in which God needed to teach me the most important lessons of my life.

As I slowly rebooted my mindset, I saw my path. I realized the world didn't revolve around me. I thought about my aunt who said maybe this was someone else's lesson, and I was merely a conduit to their growth. I vowed to judge people less and to lower my expectations. I decided to forgive my body. I let go of any trivial arguments and misunderstandings with friends. I accepted that no one has a perfect life. I searched for signs of hope wherever I could. I embraced leading with compassion. I fostered empathy toward loved ones and strangers. I didn't know where this road was taking me, but I became determined to cultivate a life full of love.

MANIFESTING COMPASSION

If you are hurt or unwell, it seems as if nothing is in your control. For me, a good day or bad day was now being decided by my body and not what I had in mind. There seemed to be so many factors out of my control, from how fast it'd take to heal to how much pain I was feeling to who was able to help me on that day, to the mood I woke up in. I don't love being out of control, but years into this journey I was learning that living with compassion was one of the few tools I had the ability to control. Like a muscle, compassion became stronger the more I practiced it. I would notice the moments I didn't feel like showing concern or empathy, and actively tried to turn it around, purposefully looking for moments to help others throughout my day.

I realized it was unfair to expect people to understand where I came from if they hadn't walked in my shoes. Can you truly understand discrimination if you haven't been discriminated against? Can you understand pain if you haven't been in pain? Can you understand the death of a parent if your parents are alive? No, you may not understand, but you can *want* to understand and actively work to do something about it.

Compassion is more than *concern* for someone fighting an illness, going through a divorce, or the loss of a loved one. *Great Good Magazine*, a science journal out of Berkeley, states that the word compassion literally means to "suffer together." Their article "What is Compassion?" states that emotion scientists define the word as "the feeling that arises when you are confronted with another's suffering and feel motivated to relieve that suffering.[1]" Compassion then is an actual call to action. It goes beyond empathy and straight into warrior mode.

I've learned that the journey to more compassionate living is going through our day-to-day lives valuing each person we come across and remembering that everyone has a story that is important. I worked in the diamond industry for more than thirty-five years. During that time, I sold millions of dollars' worth of diamonds, often sight unseen, to customers from all over the globe. For me, I wasn't just selling diamonds but was fulfilling a need. I spent the time getting to know my customers and building relationships. My strategy was never to push the most expensive diamond, but to ask the most relevant question. Who is this person, why do they want to buy jewelry, who is it for, and what impact could a diamond have on this scenario/relationship? The more questions I asked, the more interest I showed in their life and the more I sold. Cultivating compassion became valuing their story, and the result was genuine connections that had clients coming back to me year after year.

I have discovered that by showing others compassion, I gain compassion too. If I want more love in my life, I have to give more love. To have strong relationships, you have to put in the time by asking questions and learning their needs. I challenge everyone, including myself, to practice the art of active listening. Ask more questions and do more listening.

1. "What is Compassion?" *Greater Good Magazine,* https://greatergood. berkeley.edu/topic/compassion/definition#:~:text=While%20empathy% 20refers%20more%20generally,include%20the%20desire%20to%20help Accessed 11 April 2022.

Think of giving to others without expecting anything in return. There is something about focusing on others (especially if they are in need) that alleviates pain and fear. The more we give, the more we end up getting back.

When you act out of a compassionate place, your world becomes better. Your pain starts to make sense. You lead with love in your heart and get to watch the ripple effects flitter across your universe. When you are in pain, thinking of others gets you to focus on something beyond yourself When you show compassion to others, you learn the skills needed to help yourself.

You Matter

When I would give a sales talk to a conference crowd, I always ended by saying, "What you do matters. Everyone matters." I wanted to remind the audience that there is beauty and hope inside us all. Whether you believe in God or take solace knowing that we have stardust inside our bodies, we are all connected. I happen to believe God is in each of us; a key piece of information that inspires me to see each human in front of me as a glorious creation with purpose. That goes for *you* too. Whatever your beliefs, you must remember that your life has meaning no matter what.

Your life is still meaningful if you're in pain and on the couch. You make a difference in the world—despite the turmoil in your life—every time you reach out to a friend in need. It matters for everyone if you respect yourself enough to look for meaning in your day-to-day life. I know full well that when you're in pain, it's hard to see beyond your suffering, but if you can get quiet and focus on what is essential in your world, your perspective will change. When you try to see the best in yourself and others, sympathy and kind heartedness take over feelings of anger, betrayal, or jealousy.

Recovering after my surgeries, I struggled with doubts and questions about my worth in the world. I wasn't working, didn't have children to look after, and had lost my social support of being active with my sporty friends. It was a struggle to find meaning in the mundane of recovery time and time again. On the days where I wanted to give up, I found that every time I flexed my compassion muscle, I felt stronger emotionally. When I reached out to friends or offered encouragement to someone in my online support group, I felt better. I felt stronger. I knew I still mattered.

I will forever be learning how to be more compassionate but have noticed that sometimes compassion is as easy as just listening, just showing up and listening. While researching new potential solutions for my pain, I became part of a SI joint fusion Facebook support group. I posted a bunch of questions about this surgery, and a woman named Julie responded, and eventually hopped on the phone with me to share her experience of battling through sixteen surgeries. She so patiently shared all she's discovered through the journey and encouraged me to keep seeking out answers and make a plan. She was such a calm soul, and I just knew that I could call her anytime and she would be there for me, which was huge. She then connected me to others who had been on a similar path as me. One of which was a young man named Jonny, who had been a professional dancer, but had a back injury that prohibited him from returning to his career. He'd been through a back fusion, like me, and then had an SI joint fusion on both sides of his body. He was spending his days in a wheelchair, and though I know he won't stay in that wheelchair forever, it was a harsh reality for him to not just be able to get up and dance like he always had. Dance had been his joy and antidote to pain, and now he had to find a different solution.

After hearing his story, I was determined to regularly reach out to him on the phone to ask him to share how he was doing week after week. I would check on him in a text or a phone call. When I got him on the phone, my goal was to just listen, and in those moments, I could feel the huge compassion I had for him, and he had for me. This was a level I never would've had before my own experience with pain. There's no way in my past life I could've carved out hours in my week to speak with a stranger, and to not be distracted by all the other things I had to do in my life. Now, I could be on the phone for hours and feel like that was the most important act I could be doing.

These phone calls were full of learning and healing. The healing came from knowing there are people going through similar things myself. The learning came from the vulnerability of others sharing how they made it through each day. Having experienced such severe pain myself, I could feel what they were going through. Now, at the forefront of my mind, were all the people in this world who are in pain. In my prayers I put people in pain as the focus. and I especially prayed for those in pain who are by themselves and struggling on their own. I just hate that for people, and out of that hate comes an extraordinary amount of love for them that I honestly didn't know I was capable of.

I was lucky to have found Mayo as my medical homebase. No matter where you are getting help, it's important to create a team and to feel like your healthcare providers are your partners in getting better. Going through multiple surgeries, I learned I had new capacities for empathy and compassion beyond what I'd ever experienced. I came in with a broken back and left with new tools for connecting to others' suffering. The doctors and the nurses had so much empathy that I learned by example and practiced such tools with my fellow patients. They taught me that part of your healing is learning to help others (even on your worst days). We all need to learn to walk with our eyes up, and to realize that even at our lowest point, there is someone else suffering more.

When you share compassion from your heart, it helps relieve suffering, if only for a few precious moments. I don't have to have great wealth, perfect health, or wear a medal in order to show compassion, and have come to know that the greatest heroes are those who walk daily with compassion as a core value. I have been blessed to be both the recipient and student of such powers. It's so easy not to engage, to be in your own pain where you can't tap into anything. When you lift your eyes though, your perceptions have the ability to change, and in that change, you begin to see that everyone, even the most put together of humans, is craving connection. And connection is something we each have the power to share.

Look for the Gifts

The more we can make sense of our suffering and look for lessons and gifts, the quicker we will recover and the more compassion we will have for ourselves and others. Time is your friend, and it will slowly unravel the truths you seek and the empathy you desire. The meaning in your suffering will take time to ripen and develop, but you must have your head up and eyes open to notice the hope and find value in your pain and misery.

I know it isn't always easy to see those gifts though. I used to love the mornings, always eager and excited for a new day of opportunity. Now, in the midst of continuous years of pain, I often hate them. I hate them because they can feel so empty, and that emptiness is (ironically) so loud in our minds. On days I have things planned, it's so much easier to center myself, but those days where pain is keeping me home, it is a battle to quiet my mind enough to hear that inner voice who still believes in me. When I do get to that point in the day where I hear her, she often reminds me to "Add the gifts back into my sight line."

With that motivation, I start looking around my space blubbering out all the things I'm grateful for—that comfy pillow, clean water in a glass, Finn's toy, Finn, peanut butter, a bottle of wine from a friend, that friend from that friend group, friends in general, family, still having my mom as my warrior, neighbors, neighbors who make me laugh, laughter in general, my voice, cell phones, long talks with strangers, my roof, my ceiling fan, windows that give me a clear view of the weather before I step outside....The list can keep on going if I stay present.

The gratitude gives space In my heart to pinpoint the gifts. Extra time with my Irish lass mother. Deeper appreciation for people. Increased empathy and compassion. Grace and its ability to help me admit I'm imperfect and yet still lovable. Not taking for granted any time I show up to do hard things, knowing there is encouragement and learning that will meet me there. The fact that I am writing a book that I will share with others to help them through those hard things. The reality that even when my body is locked up, my soul can still be dreaming of the adventures I have ahead of me. Seeing how souls are strengthened during challenges, and how out of that strength comes greater love, compassion, and wisdom.

· · ·

Hope Nugget: When you act out of a compassionate place, you learn the skills needed to heal and make our world better.

Chapter 22

Own Your Story

How Do You Restart?

In order to stay resilient, it's imperative to hit the fast forward button and try to see beyond the suffering of the day. You have to look deep within in order to rebuild and start over. The truth is you need to get back on that train even if you don't know where it's going. You have to start the journey anew with those first tentative steps and know that any movement forward will build momentum and give you confidence that yes, this too shall pass, and you are strong enough to finish this race.

I see now that my suffering has forged my fiery soul into something stronger, much like a beautiful kintsugi piece. Kintsugi is a Japanese art form where breaks and cracks in an object like a plate, bowl, or vase are lovingly restored and treated as part of the object's history. *Kintsugi* means "golden journey," in Japanese, and artisans carefully mend the object's cracks with a lacquer resin mixed with platinum, gold, or silver. The kintsugi vases, artfully fixed with gold, show that broken things, even us humans, can not only be made whole again, but can be made stronger.

I think of the scars on my body as part of my "golden journey" or maybe "titanium journey" or "cobalt journey." My scars aren't universally celebrated like a gold mixture is, but I see the beauty in the way my heart has mended and become stronger. We may not feel like our scars are the equivalent of a gold laced bowl, and it's healthy to feel all the emotions of a setback or new struggle, but please know that sometimes we humans have blinders up to the beauty our scars elicit.

My mom was always the one who would look at my incision after surgery. I was too afraid to look. My mom would look at it, clean it, and take pictures to send to Mayo. After each surgery, the incision would get a little larger and a little larger and a little larger. I would ask Mom how it looked, and she'd always reply joyfully, "It looks good Pat. Not looking too bad."

She would take off the surgical mesh tape that went up and down the incision all the way from my butt crack to my bra and she would say, "Oh yeah, it's a bit bigger, but it looks good. It looks really good, Pat!" As a staple would be protruding from my back she would say, "It looks fine!" I would laugh every time, amazed that she could be so calm at a time like this, but even with Mom's reassurance, I couldn't bear to look. I couldn't accept that this was truly what my body looked like now.

One morning, I forgot to look away when a glance of my back protruded my mirror. I was changing into a swimsuit when a memory of getting ready for a school swim meet hit me, and instead of Pat the recovering patient, I was Pat the highschooler preparing for a meet. I used to always look at my back while dressing in front of a mirror because it was one of my favorite features. I always knew I had a great back, a strong back, a butterflyer swimmer's back.

I'd been too scared to see how my back had changed since surgery, but that morning my bravery went back to work. I stayed looking, taking in every centimeter of the long, red scar piercing down my back, its permanence reminiscent of a tattoo. It wasn't as terrifying as I'd built it up in my mind, many had far worse scars than I, but it still made me shudder. After the initial chills that ran up my spine, curiosity took over. This was my new back now, and it was layered with stories represented in this one resilient scar, and I should get to know it.

I began to admire my scar, knowing that scars (both internal and external) are reminders of what we've overcome. They are plot points in the journey of life, bringing us to where we are today. Knowing this, I started to become prouder the more I looked at my scar. It became my proof that I entered the ring and didn't give up.

Owning Your Story

After my second Big Kahuna surgery, I worried people were giving up on me. I had always enjoyed being a positive resource and supportive shoulder to lean on for my friends and family. Now, I was so dependent on others for support, that I could barely give any. It felt like someone took my story—the story I was living—and closed the book on me. It felt like life was giving me a huge, hard kick in the stomach that pushed me so far backward I hardly recognized myself.

My family and closest friends knew I was not an attention-seeking person when it came to my challenges. They knew if you put a microphone in my hand, I'd be up on stage ready to tell a joke or give a motivational speech without a second thought. Sharing anything where I might be pitied was my worst nightmare. But now, having been injured longer than I ever imagined, I couldn't shake the dread that I thought people were now thinking, "Here she goes again, that Pat with more bad news. She's always sick, something is always wrong." When I was perfectly healthy, I had thought the same thing about others, and the shame I feel for ever thinking such a thought is deep.

It never did me any good to obsess about what others were thinking. We all have the right to throw a pity party or just pull the covers over our heads and tune out the world. Doing that though, sacrifices the great gift we can receive of sharing our lives with others. To restart your life again, you can only wallow in the muck of fear, loneliness, and depression for a short time. Give yourself a limit: a day, the weekend, a week. *Today is awful, and I'm going to allow all my emotions and worries to surface, but tomorrow I will do something that will help my recovery.*

That can look like walking one lap around your block, participating in a hobby that brings you joy, or reaching out for support from a friend.

I'm human so there were many days where I cut everyone out and could only cry and ask, *Why me?* It was only after the tears dried up and my voice became less hoarse, that clarity came back into my brain, telling me that in order to heal, I needed to *own* my story (even if I didn't want to). I couldn't change that my body failed me, but I could change how it defined me. We can't control cancer or

249

our backs giving out, but we can handle our setbacks and reframe our narrative. By owning what happened to us, we can slowly gain strength and confidence.

This makes me think of one of my favorite pieces of wisdom from Brene Brown: "You may not have signed up for a hero's journey, but the second you fell down, got your butt kicked, suffered a disappointment, screwed up, or felt your heart break, it started. It doesn't matter whether we are ready for an emotional adventure—hurt happens."

I'll be honest. I'm so freaking sick and tired of talking about my hurt. I know that pain isn't me, and that there's much more to my story than my physical setbacks, but I also don't want to ignore the larger story just because I don't like certain parts of it. It's a daily chore to work on cultivating the courage to be vulnerable and authentic, but it's crucial. Doing so has taught me to transition my focus from what I think other people want to hear from me, to simply telling them the truth. Along the way I've learned my voice has different nuances, lilts, and capacity than I ever knew.

That one moment, when my back gave out on a random April day in my house, changed me. It changed me because it brought to the surface all the things I'd taken for granted. It changed me because my story now had to pivot in ways I'd never imagined. I thought I'd swing a tennis racquet until I was eighty, and now I was having to rewrite that story. The truth is, all of us at one time or another have to rewrite our story.

In the very beginning of my injury, I used to have a hard time telling this version of my story. I always cried whenever

I began explaining it, and thus avoided it whenever possible. The only people I felt safe to disclose everything to were my closest friends and family who were there to listen so encouragingly. As trial after trial took place, this close circle encouraged me to be journaling my experiences. "Pat, what's happening to you is crazy and could be a book!" I kept hearing this over and over again from the humans I most trusted, and it began to stick as I made the decision to actually transfer my journal entries into a book for others. It felt like a nudge that what I was going through would be worth it someday.

Of course, I doubted time and time again whether or not anyone would want to read this and was still timid about sharing my story. Was I kidding myself, desperate to find meaning in my pain, to think someone else would care to read about it?

On the fourth anniversary of my incident, I decided to post a section from the first chapter of the book to Facebook. I was nervous to share my words with so many other people, and I knew it would kill me if it received no response, but I mustered up the courage anyway. What's life for if not to do something that scares the crap out of you every once in a while? I clicked "post" and then set my social media away, trying not to obsess about how my story would be received.

After a few hours, I couldn't help but check on it, and was stunned by the amazing responses I was getting. Hundreds of comments and private messages were flooding in from people saying that they needed to hear what I'd shared that day. People were telling me that upon hearing my story, they were inspired to become stronger. It was a moment that changed everything for me.

Ever since, people consistently come up to me in a

parking lot or send me a message to talk with me about their pain. They often don't even know why they're sharing this with me, but say they just felt inspired to. Whenever this happens, I am floored, and yet feel like this is part of my purpose now. Pain is a universal human experience, and when you're able to share your pain, others become more willing to open up about theirs because they know you'll understand.

It's a gift that I am able to make time to listen and to share my own thoughts and nuggets of hope I've gained on the pain train. I am not a therapist nor am I a counselor. I am just someone that's been through hell and back who can connect with someone else who is currently in hell. I am always honored to be a confidante for so many stories, and whenever I feel fear about sharing my own, I remind myself of the catalyst that's occurred since I opened up my voice. By sharing my story, I am doing something right with the hand that I've been dealt. Now, my favorite rewrite in my story is how, by sharing it, I've been able to hear so many others.

We too often let the negative voices get in the way of who we are meant to be, but we must remember that nobody has the exact same story as we do. Each story is woven in the universe in a beautiful way. The greatest threat to our purpose is feeling like our story has already been told when it absolutely hasn't. We have an obsession with being 100% unique, but the greatest lesson I've learned is that humans are not so different from one another. The only way we find that out though is to connect through telling our authentic story.

I know how hard it is to believe during our hardest moments that we have something in our story worth sharing with the world, but these are the truths I've realized about every single person I've come across. These are the truths about you:

- You have a story that inspires others. Share it.
- You are going to go through tough times. Everyone is going through something.
- You have a strength that will only be fully realized in the midst of challenges. When life is at its hardest, do not forget that you are stronger than you know.
- You are a success, and it shows every time you choose love over hate, kindness over anger, gratitude over bitterness.
- You are constantly learning and growing. Who you were is not who you are now, and who you will be in the future is not who you are now.
- You are seen. You are heard. You matter.
- You are not just a number but an intentional human being with a specific purpose and every day is a chance to go toward that, and to find joy in this life.
- You can get out of the rabbit holes you find yourself in.
- Your toughest moments are temporary.
- You have the ability to endure anything.
- You show up and do hard things.
- You have people who are here for you and care for you, even when it doesn't seem like it.

Please take these truths and allow them to fuel a grace in the way you look at your story. With that grace as a shield from the harshest voices, don't be afraid to share it. The way to healing is the empowering act of sharing your story in a safe space. This brave move responds like a match, igniting a universe of understanding. The world needs you in it so don't be afraid to own your story and please find a way that resonates with your soul, to share it.

Hope Nugget: Sharing your story is a power move. You never know what doors or relationships may open by simply sharing your authentic story with others.

Chapter 23

Silver Linings

It always comes back to my mom for me. In the Spring of 2022, she developed a serious urinary tract infection that was just not going away. My sisters had been taking turns being my mom's nurse, and now it was my time. I knew my mom was in a bad way because when I asked for the latest update, my sisters said, "To give you an indication, Pat, she has no makeup on and she's living in her pjs."

My mom always looked ready for a glamor photo shoot no matter the circumstance, so this was serious. I remember not too long ago, Mom was preparing to have a surgery. This was in between two of my surgeries, and I was ready to take care of mom after everything she did for me. We had to be there at five a.m. and arrived right on time. I waited patiently in the waiting room throughout her procedure until a doctor came out and told me she was awake and now in the post-op room where I could go in and see her. I went in and the nurses were coming in and out and every time they came in, they kept telling my mom how beautiful she looked. Wow, she just had surgery and she looked so beautiful! Who does that? I looked at her though, and I agreed. She always looked good, even after surgery.

After yet another nurse came in and made a comment about how gorgeous she looked, I took a closer glance, and I realized my mom was in full makeup. She must've woken up at three or four a.m. to put full makeup on before surgery.

"Mom, you have makeup on."

"Well, yeah."

"You're not supposed to put on makeup for major surgery. Why on earth did you

put makeup on?"

She answered, "'Cause they didn't tell me I couldn't put makeup on."

"Mom, everyone knows you don't put on makeup for major surgery."

"Well, they didn't tell me I couldn't, so I did."

That's who my mom is. No matter what, she looked great. My surgeons at Mayo have always loved my mom. If I came to an appointment without her, they would ask, "Where's your mom? How is she doing?" Not, "What's new with you, Pat?" It was my mom they were interested in. If I ever post a picture of my mom on social media, she gets three hundred more likes than a picture of just me. Everyone who meets her is drawn to her. She is a living saint with unshakeable faith, who at the same time, uses humor to keep us all laughing. I'm realizing she is a hero to everyone she knows, but to me, she is the greatest hero that's ever lived (I don't care if that sounds cheesy).

As I drove the fifteen-hour drive from Austin to Des Moines in one shot, knowing she wasn't making any effort with her appearance, I was incredibly anxious about what she would be like when I arrived. To ease my nerves, my mind started wandering to the last time I'd seen her in person—her ninetieth birthday.

September 2nd, 2021 was mom's ninetieth birthday and we had a beautiful outdoor celebration with most of our family in attendance, many of them surprising her. We hired a young troupe of Irish dancers to perform for her, and mom's giant smile lit up as she witnessed the fast, precise movements of each dancer's feet bouncing up and down in perfect rhythm. The troupe offered to teach the group an Irish jig and my mom was the first one up, dragging most of the family up there with her. Even at ninety, my mom is the epitome of spunk.

We played lawn games, including life sized Jenga, and sang "Happy Birthday" as we handed my mom an Irish themed cake that said *Happy Birthday Mom-Grandma. We love you!* There were toasts to the birthday girl and too many jokes to not make one's abs sore. Sparklers were lit at the end of the night to conclude a full Henneberry-approved celebration.

I sat back in awe most of the time, my cheeks sore from laughing, grateful to witness the firecracker my mom truly is. As I let the joy fill my soul, I knew this was one silver lining in the hardship of my journey. All this extra time with my mom the past few years, even if it meant her cleaning my scars, placing bandages on and off, helping me off the toilet, and taking pictures of my back so I can see what it looks like, I wouldn't trade for anything.

The memories started to make me emotional as I drove. Until I was there with her in person and could do something to help, my imagination was taking off with all the worst possible scenarios. Thankfully, I was saved from myself for a bit when one of my book editors called to discuss some of the latest chapters of this book. We were in the midst of a conversation about me gearing up to finally dive into pickle-ball when out of nowhere I saw this giant billboard that I swear said *Free Pickleball* on it. I shrieked and began to read it out loud to her, but as I did, I realized it actually said *Free Pickle Bar!* We both burst out laughing, and if I hadn't been in a rush I would've probably stopped at this gas station in the middle of nowhere Oklahoma with a free pickle bar to at least take a picture. I took this billboard as a sign that things were going to be okay, and that God was with me. If I've learned anything throughout my life, it is that the universe communicates with me through humor.

The pickle billboard wasn't even the craziest part of this road trip, however. Aside from Finn, I had another passenger with me—the ashes of my good friend's mother strapped safely in my front passenger seat.

Ironically, I had already been planning to head up to Iowa before I received the call that mom was not feeling well and would need extra help for a while. My good friend Mike's mother-in-law had just passed away—a woman who lived in Austin, but was originally from Des Moines, Iowa. I had been friends with Mike and his wife Cathi for over thirty years, having worked with Mike in various companies all connected to the diamond industry (we even had our own company at one point). When I found out Cathi's mom had passed, I knew I would do my darndest to be at the celebration of life in Iowa.

When my plans changed, I called Mike letting him know I would be unable to attend the celebration of life because I would need to stay with mom who was sick with a severe UTI.

"Pat, that's the exact thing Cathi's mom just passed

from," Mike told me. As I hung up the phone, my stomach was in knots. I knew UTIs were serious for the elderly, but I still didn't think about it being able to take the life of one.

Ten minutes later Cathi called me. "Hey, Pat, I'm going to ask you something, and you can totally say no."

"Go ahead. What is it?"

"Do you think you could bring my mom's ashes back to Des Moines with you when you drive up to see your mom? My mom was from Des Moines, and she wanted to be buried by her husband there. We were going to mail the ashes, but I would feel so much better if you drove them with you instead."

My life is anything but predictable.

"Of course I can do that!" I know this felt like a serendipitous miracle for Cathi and would be one less thing for her to worry about during this time of immense grieving.

So here I was on my drive with an extra companion, trying not to picture my own mother's condition, allowing myself to soak up the irony of this all. I let myself think about how life is so fragile, and our bodies so temporary. I thought about my own body and its set of challenges. Then I thought about the legacy that humans truly leave in this world. It isn't one's body that we remember, but it's a person's spirit, and their impact, that lasts forever.

I needed to humble myself that though my body might not live up to my expectations, I could still use my heart, my mind, my joy, and my humor to make others know that they matter. I could love wholeheartedly, and nothing, not even my body's failings, could take that away. My body would be a pile of ashes one day, but my soul wouldn't be. Love does not die with the body.

I couldn't bring myself to picture life after my mom goes

to heaven. It was too painful for me to even consider. I knew that whenever that day comes, I would desperately miss her presence, conversation, hugs, jokes, and wisdom. I would yearn for time with her in the flesh but would understand that her love wouldn't leave me. Even if my mom is in the worst shape I've ever seen her when this fifteen hour day is done, all the memories of her won't mean anything less. They'll mean even more. I won't love her less because of her weakness but will strengthen my heart to give sacrificially and love harder than ever.

Could that mean that others might see me in the same light? Could I see myself with that filter? Does my suffering not negate my gifts, the life I lived before surgery, and the future adventures (whatever those may be) I have ahead of me? The extra time with my mom has been the ultimate silver lining in all of this hardship, but I think it goes beyond that. That silver lining has expanded into a declaration I am beginning to believe: I am worthy of love, even in my weakness.

I know so many of my loved ones had been trying to get me to see that for years, encouraging me to give up the insecurity that I am merely a burden. But it was right then, on that unforgettable drive, with the only physical remnants left of an amazing woman next to me, that I finally got it.

P.S. My mom fully recovered from that UTI. Hallelujah!

Hope Nugget: Look for the silver linings even in your most difficult seasons. They exist to teach you the most beautiful lessons.

Chapter 24

My Miracles

Knowing *Your Soul is Well.*

They say that when one sense is taken from a human, their other senses intensify to compensate. Throughout these trials, I think that's what was happening to my soul. My physical body was failing time and time again, but my soul was gaining new strength, showing up when my body couldn't. My compassionate heart began beating more ferociously, desperately wanting to make the most of this situation in ways I never would've discovered if I hadn't had my health taken from me. I was being humbled greatly, fighting against the perfectionist in me who wanted to show everyone that I was back. I wanted to look strong and healthy on the outside, the appearances meaning more to me than I ever knew they would. Faced with this internal mirror, I realized that the only thing we can keep from decaying is our soul. Our soul is the part of us that will live on in the hearts of our family and friends. When we help one another out, it isn't the size of our muscles that makes the impact, but the power of our generous hearts in volunteering to help. That is the type of act that will change the course of a community.

There's always been this part of me that loved when people asked, "How do you do it, Pat? How do you keep showing up?" My ego wanted to believe it was because I was just that tough. The truth was, the people around me were even tougher than I. I kept showing up because other people's souls were feeding into mine.

As I've accepted my need for others, it's hit me that resilience isn't just about showing up. Other humans aren't inspiring me because they're physically present. They inspire me because they are showing up *to do hard things*. The same could be said for me. I'm not merely a face in a room showing up. When my soul is strong, I am showing up wholeheartedly to do *hard freaking things*. I don't show up to yoga class just to check it off my list. I show up to yoga knowing it is going to be a battle, knowing it is going to take every piece of my strength to do it. I am showing up not just in spite of, but *for* the hard. Deep down, I know this is the only way I am going to empower the internal pieces of me. And the only reason I know that is because I've seen so many others show up with and for me when I knew they were struggling in their own lives. This is how we all get strength—by showing up together. This is how our souls blossom and carry weight we couldn't have thought possible before.

When I competed in triathlons I hated the running section. I was a terrible runner so when it was this part of the trifecta, I always felt discouraged. There would be times when I would approach a hill and just stop moving, not believing I could go any farther. Then a stranger would come along and pat me on the back and say, "You've got this!"

Suddenly my legs would feel like they'd just been electro-cuted with energy, and I'd start running again.

This has happened so many times in my life, and it was only through this painful journey, where I've stopped and forced myself to reflect, that I've realized these moments were people sharing their souls with me. For healing to take place we have to open our being to others so that we can be filled, and vice versa. There's no way we can keep going without others. We have to be open to the pat on our back.

My dear friend Anne, a fellow Irish lass who I consider a sister, called me every day for years throughout my surgeries and recoveries. She always took my calls, but if I didn't call, she'd be the one punching my number into her phone and checking on my soul that day, always ready with wisdom, good humor, and a present, listening ear. This is how she showed up for me and is part of why I keep going day after day.

What if I had just shut down, and never received the encouragement others had to give? Would I still be stuck on that hill during a triathlon, wallowing in regret? What if I didn't answer Anne's calls? What if I wasn't open to physical therapy, or my surgeon's advice? What if I wasn't willing to put my ego aside to help me show up?

I can confidently say I would be going nowhere. As I've accepted the souls from friends or strangers, I've become braver, gained more courage, and allowed myself to open up and hope.

Though it took a life altering event for me to get to this place, we don't have to wait for a crisis in order to open up our souls to others. Trust me. There are plenty of people out there right now who are ready and willing to come alongside you, even when you don't believe it. The face you see in the mirror isn't always the face others see. Those beautiful humans who live daily with compassion see you beyond the surface and they can teach you to do the same.

Look at your soul. Are you proud of it? If not, don't be afraid to change. There is always time and grace for you. The answer most likely is in whether or not you have the courage to invest in others and allow others to do the same for you.

I get that it's easier said than done. In my worst moments, where I was on the ground writhing in pain, I wasn't thinking about how I could show up for others or how others would be there for me if I let them. I was merely surviving. For months, when this whole thing started, I was afraid to turn off the lights. I kept repeating a narrative that I was alone, and it just increased whenever I turned the lights off to the point where I couldn't stand it. I thought I had no choice but to sleep with the lights on forever. It took me about six months to trust and believe that I would be okay in the dark. Part of this was trusting that my soul would be okay, which I only began to believe after soul after soul was there for me. Having made it through such turbulent times I knew I could make it through more. I think we all need to know we are okay in dark places. They won't last forever. There will be a light we can turn on eventually, most likely inspired by the spark of another soul. I know I am only still here because of the generosity and action of my neighbors, friends, healthcare workers, and a plethora of strangers who showed me empathy beyond what I expected.

Sometimes it's difficult to even know if your soul is well or not. I always thought my soul felt good when I was doing physically or mentally well, but was I really checking in? Now, I am determined to make sure it is up to the task when I am not doing great in those arenas. So how can I know if my soul is well? For me, these are the measurables that allow me to know if my soul is well or not:

1. I see others beyond myself and am able to show them compassion and empathy.
2. I accept help and know it is important to do so.
3. I have a desire to be there for others, even if I'm forced to do so in a limited capacity.
4. I feel gratitude for the little things.
5. I say yes to being around people.
6. I look for signs of hope.
7. I dream.
8. I am unafraid of the silence or the dark and use it to pray, breathe, and notice beauty.

I encourage all of us to make it a habit to check in with our soul regularly. It's only then that true transformation can burst into action.

Creating Your Own Team

I talk in team terminology frequently. This is because I've learned that no matter what you are facing, you need to create your own team. I'm still learning this, constantly adding new people to my team, and realizing the foundation of healing is honoring that we weren't meant to do life alone. We like to tell ourselves we are capable of overcoming our struggles on our own, but when you break that theory down, it just doesn't make sense. We are relational beings. Think of the best memories of your life. Most often there was at least one person alongside you. We all need cheerleaders, shamans, comedians, straight shooters, and good old fashioned, loyal friends in our lives.

Creating a team means you will need to advocate for yourself. You know what you need. You might have to be the team leader, you might need to be the one to *ask* for help, and that's perfectly okay. In fact, that can be great! Seek out the best heart surgeon or cancer specialist you can get. Try and make everyone you meet—from the receptionist and nurses to the blood drawers and physical therapists—members of your team. Sometimes just by being kind, even when you're feeling the worst, can make medical practitioners' defenses break down.

When you do life alone, it can feel like you've been swimming six hours in the open water where the current picks up, the waves get bigger, and you still have a couple of miles to go. Every part of you is exhausted, you don't think you can go on much longer, and you're convinced the water is going to envelop you at any moment.

Having an amazing team around you combats that feeling, and allows you to stop focusing on your stroke, and instead set your mind on the shore where your friends are, and the finish line is. You begin to hear their cheers, which are so loud that they distract you, summoning you to the end where you celebrate with a large glass of wine and a lot of laughs that make you forget the pain you just went through (at least for a moment).

When I left for my first big kahuna surgery, I knew I was going to be gone for a long time, and when you're out of sight you can be out of mind due to everything people have going on in their life. Though I found it hard to believe that people weren't thinking of me at every moment of the day, I knew this would be the case. This is why having a head coach (mine was my mom) is so important. They are there as your number one and are never going to miss a beat when it comes to you.

My main physical therapist, Ian, was one of my first string players. He always encouraged me with positivity. When a nerve or something was in the wrong spot, I would come to him basically crawling into his clinic, dragging my legs, walking with my canes and a desperate look on my face. I would look up at him and immediately start bawling. He would sit down with me, and confidently say, "Don't worry. You're going to get through this, Pat. It's just a hard day that you will overcome. I'm going to help you."

My team at Mayo—Dr. Huddleston, the PA Stacy, and the surgical team (I don't know their names or even full faces, but I know their eyes) are also first stringers. One of the surgical assistants was there for three of my surgeries, and she held my hand each time, assuring me it would all turn out okay.

If I didn't have many of my core team members: my nephews, sisters, and brother-in-law, I would not have made it. My neighbors are a huge part of my team as well as every friend who picks up the phone to check on me.

I had to build a team for my recoveries in Des Moines, finding a new community of physical therapists—Kristy and Lindsey. I adored them as well as their head administrator, Judy, who was so valuable to me, always helping me put my schedule together with more patience than I knew was possible.

My mom's neighbors, who I barely knew, would bring food over to me, always checking in, or even taking care of Finn at times when I had to go back to Mayo and Mom insisted on coming with me. These were all people I didn't know very well who rallied for me and they all became part of my team.

Every six to seven months I was rebuilding my life, going back to Austin, and being met with a lot of new faces, as well as many of the old ones I was always so happy to see. My Yogis are team members who always greet me with compassion and understand I'm battling through another recovery, but don't baby me. I go swim my laps at the pool and there are new people to meet, adorned with smiles that welcome me into the water. They are also added to the team.

An example of this took place on the fifth anniversary of when my lumbar shifted from my spine. I was proud of myself that I showed up to Vinyasa yoga at noon. It was a hard day to show up to anything, as this is an anniversary I don't love to mark, but knew I needed to. The yoga teacher, Lauren, played an awesome soundtrack throughout the class. Every single song felt relevant and brought tears to my eyes as I flowed through all the different moves, in my corner, holding onto the wall occasionally, but feeling strong and good.

I went home after that and tried to focus a little bit on some work but was having trouble as the day dragged on. I called Mom and ended up getting a little emotional with her and could feel myself getting close to a deep funk. Before I got too deep into that, I felt a stirring that I needed to show up to the pool at my gym.

That's what my soul was craving, and I decided to listen to her. I gathered my swim bag, goggles, and wonderful earbuds where I can listen to music as I swim, and then drove over to the pool. It felt amazing as my skin hit the chlorine and the water seeped over my body. I started swimming and could feel it was the right move. I cried as I listened to songs that helped me reflect on the past five years and the five surgeries that went with them.

After swimming fifteen hundred yards, I stopped to take a breath, hoping that I could also shake off some of the painful memories that were on repeat in my mind. I noticed a guy coming to swim laps in the lane next to me. He had a warmth about him that put me at ease. We smiled, said hi to each other, and then went on to swim in our designated lanes.

Eventually, my body (and soul) told me that I'd done enough laps for the day. As I went to leave, I told the guy next to me to have a good day, and then he came closer to introduce himself. At the same time, we both said, "My name's Pat." I experienced a split second of shock, and then we busted up laughing. On this difficult day, I was meeting another Pat. *Of course.* My brain immediately went into this ah-ha moment where I thought, *Oh my gosh, this guy's name is Pat and he is like this soul angel sent to swim next to me today and encourage me. I just know it.*

We both got out, talking as we packed up our stuff. We were in a deep conversation about swimming and how important it is to show up even on the days we aren't feeling it, when I blurted out, "Today is my five-year anniversary of five surgeries in five years. Today was so important for me to show up."

He responded by giving me a huge hug, and when he let go, asked me about my journey. We talked for a while as I recounted my story and learned some of his, inspired by tales

269

of his wife—a wonderful novelist who he was proud of. The conversation continued as we walked to the parking lot. As our eyes welled with tears, more hugs were shared, and it was this perfect moment where both souls wholeheartedly showed up.

This was a stranger (turned angel) named Pat and he filled my soul that night by showing up, giving me a hug, and listening. I knew it was no coincidence that my soul had urged me to go to the pool tonight. I was meant to meet this Pat and be reminded that there was still hope for me yet. It affirmed the truth that there are a lot of strangers out there willing to be on your team as a listener of your story, willing to give a hug or high five or a *pat* on the back.

Every single surgery I added more people to my team. My team now includes the Benedictine sisters who I say the rosary with once a month on Zoom. I added Finn to my team. Finn, the waterboy, always by my side. Finn was there for my hip surgery and when they took out my rods and screws and will be there for the rest of it. My assistant coaches, of course, are Monica from Benedictine, who is always right alongside me as we help each other get through our pain journeys; and my sisters who always show up for my surgeries and to help Mom and me.

A lot of people on my team don't necessarily need to know my whole situation and they may not know they're even on the team, but I hold a space for them on my bench. They're a huge part of my healing even if they are unaware. Some of these are individuals I've met in Facebook support groups. Some are podcast creators or authors of books that reminded me of a lesson I needed just at the right moment. Some are strangers who have called me back when I've asked them questions about a surgery they've already had. Like Julie, who reached out to me and talked with me for almost two hours about her experience with a surgery I was researching. These are people who don't even know me but give me emotional support.

Ultimately, what I've learned is that it is important to keep growing your team as it's never a full team. This is how you continue to trudge through it all. Each member of the team is one of your miracles.

Speaking of miracles, I am amazed by the bond between my mom and Finn. Whenever I stay with Mom in Iowa, Finn comes along, and he thrives. In the morning, Mom and Finn open the front door and look out to see what kind of day it will be. One time, I was sitting in the living room, and had my phone in my hand. As they went on their daily weather observation trek, I had the perfect angle to take a picture of the back of them. Finn staring straight ahead and Mom leaning her head down as she talked to Finn about what they were seeing on a particularly sunny day.

I posted the picture on social media and all my friends loved it. My good friend Kelly's husband, Craig Anderson, is an award-winning watercolor artist. He loved the picture I posted so much that he painted a beautiful watercolor of the image and gifted it to me, which hangs proudly in my home as a reminder of the two souls who showed up for me when I needed someone most.

A Beautiful Reminder

It was six months post the rods and screws being taken out and it was the 2023 Super Bowl. The Philadelphia Eagles were playing the Kansas City Chiefs. I went to school in Kansas and being a Midwestern gal, the Chiefs were my team. My best friend Anne grew up in Philadelphia and has always been a huge Eagles fan. I went to Anne and her partner Sarah's home to watch the game. They have three standard poodles, one of which is a puppy, and Finn loves to play with these cousins of his.

I was having extreme pain on and off my SI Joint since my surgery (and even before) and had been waiting three months to get an appointment with a world-renowned SI Joint surgeon at Mayo. Shortly after I arrived at Anne and Sarah's ready to watch some football, my left leg began going into some major nerve convulsions. I couldn't control my leg and the pain was killing me.

It was nice to be around friends as this was happening as these are some friends who during the past few years were always accommodating, never missing a beat, and never treating me any differently. They would often invite me over for dinner, even though I accepted their invitation with conditions: "I can come but I will have to stand." They never acted like it was a problem, and happily stood at the kitchen counter with me as we ate the delicious meals they always cooked.

That Super Bowl night was no different. They immediately got me ice, helped me lay on my side, and made jokes while watching the football game. When I needed to use the bathroom, they helped me up and basically carried me to the loo. I was so grateful not to be alone during this moment. Had I been home alone, I know I would've gone down a terrible mental rabbit hole and spent the day crying. It was so much easier to get through this with friends by my side.

The next day, I called Anne to thank her and Sarah for all they've done for me, and how much the day before had meant to me. During this conversation, Anne said that she and Sarah had discussed it and that neither one of them thought they could handle the kind of pain I was going through. Though I assured her, she probably could, it felt nice to be validated in the fact that what I'm going through does suck. We talked about my upcoming trip back to Mayo to meet this new surgeon, and before the call ended, Anne said, "Maybe this is your miracle, Pat. Maybe this meeting is your miracle."

My eyes welled up with tears when I heard this sentence. I'd honestly forgotten that a miracle was even possible still. It was too easy for me to get in my head and give up on such hopeful thinking. But here was my dear friend, reminding me of the truth that at any moment a miracle could pop up. Why not hope that this could be the one I was looking for? Even if it didn't look like an obvious miracle, since miracles often don't come easy, I could help tee up the miracle by at least being open to it. I could remind myself of all the miracles that God had already given me from my family to Finn to the beautiful community I kept building wherever I went. This was the momentum I needed before I headed back to Mayo again.

Hope Nugget: Our soul shows up because others' souls come alongside us! Our team will

273

help us believe that tomorrow might produce a miracle.

Chapter 25

The Enigma of the End

While writing this book, I faced countless insecurities, especially concerning my story's conclusion. I've read and loved so many books where people faced huge obstacles but, in the end, had a clear victory. My ending though, is blurry. I haven't finished the race. In fact, I can't even see the finish line anymore. This is new for me because in the past, I've always known where the finish line was. I had my eye on it. When I made the last turn around the gigantic orange buoy during an open water race, I would always lift my head out of the water to find the shore. Or coming in on the last leg of the triathlon (the run, which was not my best event), I'd strain to see the finish line, hoping it was just around the corner. The finish line was always further than I thought, but once I had my eye on it, that's all I could think about. Even when it never seemed to get closer, I kept pushing and pushing until I was convinced I couldn't push any further. This always seemed to happen right before I got to the section where they have ropes, and crowds of

Pat Henneberry

people cheering us competitors on. That's the best feeling. And it made me so ecstatic that I never gave up.

I've had a plethora of rough days though where I'm exhausted from my inability to see an end in sight. Every time I think there is an answer to my struggle, pain rears its head again, and another potential surgery is recommended. This has impacted my ability to tell this story. Why would anyone want to read a book full of hardship only to reach the book's end and realize that the hardship doesn't disappear?

Varying circumstances kept pushing back the completion of this book, and a part of me kept hoping that was a sign I should hold out for a clear ending. I wished for a miracle to take place, one that would hold up to the triumphant conclusion I always pictured this book having.

Here we are at the end though, and it's completely different than what I expected. I'm on track to have my sixth surgery in five years. Not ideal. The one thing going for me is that this book is a documentation of my authentic experience. Maybe that's enough for me. Maybe that's enough for others.

The more people I meet, the more I realize that most humans don't have perfectly wrapped stories with beautiful bows placed on top. Nope. Most of us have a story where the wrapping paper we cut out doesn't quite fit right, and the tape isn't keeping the paper in place, so we keep placing more and more tape on it, hoping it'll eventually pass as acceptable. We get frustrated until we stop and realize it isn't the packaging that's important, but the gift underneath. That's what I'm holding onto. Though a victory isn't appearing on the outside, the powerful reflections and revelations I've had space to see are underneath and no one can take those away from me.

As I think of all the people I know who are struggling as they do the hard things, I see inside them the strength of warriors. If a stranger passed them on the street, they may write them off, but I know better. I know these resilient souls are the heroes of our world. Hollywood often reams us with protagonists that most anyone would aspire to, but I know that the wisest, kindest, most compassionate beings are the ones who have a story the common human wouldn't volunteer for.

I understand the traditional thinking—no one wants to suffer—but I hope to look at my story differently. I'm working to be grateful that I am one of these people, one with a story no one would want, and I am going to take my circumstances and find purpose there (whether or not I receive a movie worthy ending). This is my next mountain to climb, and not just for me, but for the millions of others whose life did not go according to plan, who had something sacred ripped away from them, who have wrestled with the idea of justice and can't understand why they're the ones with this reality. I see them, and if that's your story, I see you too. Thus, I will end this book not with a story about a change in circumstances, but one of a change in heart.

I was back at the Mayo clinic again searching for answers. My pain was increasing *again*, and I could no longer walk on my own, using my hiking poles to get around (I thought hiking poles looked more badass than a cane did). I was there to meet with a new surgeon, and to trudge through the muddy waters of tests, MRIs, CT scans, and check-ins to see if there was anything else they could do to help me. Anxiety filled every pore of my skin, like the way goosebumps cover my arms in the cold. Every time I went to Mayo, I came out needing another surgery and I didn't want another one. I wanted a simpler answer.

Worse than my fear of surgery though was my fear that the Mayo Team would put up their hands in surrender, stating there was nothing else they could do for me. While there, I also had a check-up with my surgeon Dr. Huddleston. I shakily told Dr. Huddleston how I was progressing, and ended up blurting out, "I'm such a mess and I don't know if you can do anything. Are you going to give up on me?"

He looked straight in my eyes and calmly answered, "I am not going to give up on you but honestly, at this point, most people give up. And *you* can't give up. You *can't* give up. Don't give up, Pat."

"I won't." If for no other reason than to not let this man who had invested so much into my recovery down, I wouldn't give up.

I have an affinity for funny T-shirts, and on this Mayo trip I packed a few to give me something to make me smile. On that first day of check-ins and tests, I wore a shirt that said *Tell your dog I say hi*. As I passed strangers at the clinic, all clad in masks due to the safety measures required because of the COVID-19 virus, I could see them smile with their eyes. One of the hardest parts of COVID for me was not being able to see people's smiles (the smile of a stranger always makes my day), but it forced me to learn the smile of the eyes.

The next day the text on my T-shirt of choice was *My dog thinks I'm cool*. While waiting for some medication at the Mayo pharmaceutical lab, a couple of women came up to me laughing and told me how great my shirt was. No one is in a position to laugh at Mayo, but throughout the day nurses, patients, and family members waiting for their loved ones smiled, laughed, and chatted with me all because of a silly T-shirt and it filled me up.

On my last day, I debated wearing one of the funny shirts. The past two days of appointments, meetings, and tests had left me feeling exhausted and a little hopeless. Was it inauthentic to wear something on the outside that did not reflect the state on the inside? My internal dialogue debated itself in circles, so much so that I screamed and threw myself on my hotel bed in tears. As I worked on my self-soothing, I asked myself, *who do you want to be Pat?* I replayed the memories of the past couple of days and let myself see the miracle it was of bonding with other humans in the midst of a pandemic. Clad in masks, humanity was making a habit of fearing one another, keeping our heads down, and socializing on very restricted terms. Though this was for our safety, it had side effects on the heart. Now I'd found a way to bring some joy to others by merely wearing a T-shirt. How selfish was it to not wear one? And how stupid. I needed that joy as much as the next person. Even if the shirt didn't genuinely reflect how I was feeling, it could be used as motivation for the best version of myself I wanted to be.

With my decision made, I sat up, wiped the tears away, and reached for the last silly T-shirt I'd brought with me. It had been a gift from my sister Joanne. I headed to Mayo and was immediately greeted by the chuckles of strangers and a plethora of "I like your shirt" comments. As I looked down at the writing on my shirt, I couldn't help but giggle. It said *I am only talking to my dog today.*

That day I had a check-in with my PA Stacy, who had

been with me from the beginning of my Mayo surgery. I confided in her that despite Dr. Huddleston's words, I was afraid Mayo was going to give up on my case. Stacy beamed a giant smile, looked straight at me, and said, "As long as you keep wearing those funny T-shirts, we aren't going to give up on you!" We both burst into laughter at that, and the laughter helped me to see the genuinity in her words.

After my last test of the day, I wanted to take a moment and reflect on how a week I'd been dreading turned into one I would never forget. I didn't have answers yet, but somehow I still had peace. I took a seat in the Mayo lobby, empty except for a few stragglers, and began journaling:

Here, wearing a funny T-shirt and catching the glint of a smile in the eyes of strangers I pass, I realize I am still needed. I give in to the truth that the way I am needed may change countless times over, but the reality is there is more of my story to be written.

I have spent hours and hours hating the interruptions of the life I was building. I have questioned it. I have cried, yelled, and even maniacally laughed over it. Those are all natural reactions. Yet sometimes, I have this glimmer that the Divine is doing something beautiful with all of this. In those moments, I surrender to the fact that I can be used even when I feel useless. I can move forward even when taking a physical step is painful. I can have hope even when I get my 5th call to surgery. I can be interrupted and allow that interruption to show me I'm not just my job or my finish time in a triathlon or my ability to be independent. I am someone who is figuring out who she is without all of that. I am someone who can be interrupted and not be defeated. While my back is being re-fused time and time again, my body constantly having to adapt to intrusions, my soul is going through a transformation too.

Some days I am frustrated. Some days hope feels distant.

But other days, I am wearing a "I am only talking to my dog today" T-shirt and strangers are making eye contact with me and laughing. And in this moment, I know God isn't done with me yet.

Hope Nugget: If you have breath in your lungs, God isn't done with you yet.

Epilogue: Dear Rebel

"If a bird believes it is an eagle long enough, it will eventually end up soaring like one."
—Matshona Dhliwayo

Dear Rebel,

So many people will do their best to define you. They will look at you as a docile bird. They will think you are small and that they know your limits. But they don't. I give you full permission to rebel from the borders others will put around you. Only you can determine what a healthy recovery will look like for you. Healing comes in so many different forms, and I ask that you always allow yourself space to draw outside the lines, to climb a mountain in order to get a different perspective, and to question the defined measurables, knowing there are parts of you that are impossible to weigh externally.

You will most likely face moments where your life is interrupted so greatly that you have no choice but to start over. Many will look at this with pity, but please make it a strength. Please show others starting over isn't a punishment, but an opportunity. You might need to sit out at times, you may need to evaluate your relationships, you may have to create a different schedule, try new hobbies, and cry more than you thought possible. Do it. All of this resembles courage because you are choosing not to give up, but to simply shift. Shifting is the stuff all good comeback stories are made of. Shifting leads to soaring.

The world can trick you into thinking you're alone during those deep-rooted moments of transition. Please note you are not alone. As I've written this book, you have been on my mind. I don't know exactly what path life has given you. It's impossible to compare my pain and suffering to what you are experiencing. I do know though, that I'm on your team as a loyal, wholehearted cheerleader (maybe with less high kicks, but with a whole bunch of enthusiastic cheers). I've pictured your pain and struggles and then I've seen your victories. I imagine you flying high like an eagle, triumphant in ways others may not notice, but that secretly shakes up the world. Many are too busy to notice, but I feel the rumblings of the earth moving as you take steps into the new.

Whether you know it or not, we've been on this journey together. You are not alone. You will always be in my prayers and thoughts. Keep embracing your inner rebel, you badass you. Never forget how fucking strong you have been. I see you, and the life you lead is glorious.

Love,
　　Pat

Acknowledgments

To be fully transparent, writing this acknowledgments page was anxiety inducing. There are way too many people who have blessed me with the ability to make this book possible, and I am constantly adding people to that team. With that being said, I was terrified of forgetting someone. When I couldn't make my publisher wait any longer on this, I wrote this section. Please know this list isn't all encompassing, and if you are someone who contributed greatly to my life the last five years and I forgot to mention you here, please blame it on a random spell of brain fog and know that I love you dearly.

Here goes...

My sincerest gratitude goes to the following individuals who have been there for me through these five plus years and who I know will be there for me in the future:

My family. You are everything to me. Mom, there is a reason you pop up on countless pages of this book. You are my hero and a saint for always showing up for me no matter what. Carol and Joanne, my sisters, I appreciate you driving me back and forth to Mayo and not letting me do this on my own. Aunt Sister Michele Doyle, SSSF—my spiritual guide. My nephews Michael, Billy, and Bobby, and brother-in-law Bill. Also, my new niece-in-law Melanie. My family in heaven, especially my dad. All my aunts, uncles, and cousins from the Henneberry and Kaelin families. I love you all.

The Barillas Family—my heart family—Veronica, Marty, Nico, Cruz, and Beck. I can't imagine this life without each one of you.

My dearest friends. Thank you for your inspiration and guidance, and for the endless calls and support. Honorable mentions: Anne Long, Sarah Janosik, Monica Agostini, Monica Sherman-Peter and Greg Peter, Alissa Magrum, Tammy Stanley, Misty Hillin, Carmel Fasano Brantley, Liz Arreaga, Joanna Mesecke, Anne Teal, Susan Burton, Sharon Swan, Kelly Bargabos (who encouraged me to write this book and keep writing it even when I wanted to stop), Zoe King, Heidi Block, Sherri Hendricks, Gwyn, Dave and Mark Theodore, Jenny McGivney (my fellow Special Olympics coach), Laurie Campbell, Miriam Hirschberg, Bena Thomlison, Kim Marie, Laurie Fryer, Mary McGough, Cheryl Watson, Julie and Kak Hutchens, Mike and Cathi Mojica, Jennifer Heebner, Susan Stone, and Laura Sumner and Amy Creed for showing up on that first night in rehab. Sr. Jude Fitzpatrick—my friend *and* my coach. Also, a big shout out to all my mom's friends, especially Mary Jane Brady.

My Neighbors. You are like family to me. Cathy and Don Cockerham, Cyntha Choate, Marie and Bob Paterek, Cindy and Patrick Fig-Currier, Bill and Linda Robertson, Angie Thielemans and Jeff Klaas, Lisa and Greg Rhoads, Desarie and Danny Waggoner—Thank you for being with me all the way.

Mom's Neighbors. I'm amazed by all you Ashworth Estates and West Des Moines residents who took me in like I had been your neighbor for fifty years. Your kindness was a huge comfort. I especially want to express my gratitude for the Pollock family, Bill and Gwen Mitton, Marv Johnson, Connie Grignon, Sandy and Larry Smith.

My Prayer Warriors. Thank you to my Benedictine College Rosary heroes class of 1984, the School Sisters of Saint Francis, the Benedictine Sisters of Mount St. Scholastica, Emmaus Catholic Church, in Lakeway, Texas and St. Theresa Catholic Church in Des Moines, Iowa for all their ongoing prayers.

My Care Team. Thank you to my physical therapist Ian MacGregor (you know), Lesley Scott Kranz for always pushing me to stay strong in more ways than one, and the PT team at Mercy One, especially Kristi Rinderknecht.

My Mayo Team and Doctors, especially Dr. Paul Huddleston and Stacy Stackhouse. Also, everyone who keeps Mayo afloat. You are pillars of compassion. Thank you also to the city of Rochester, MN, and the Marriott Hotels who took care of my family for so many visits. You all know the meaning of hospitality.

My noon power yoga class—Amy Thompson Martin, Trish McGarrell, Larry Williams, Hway Siew Tan, Monika Grable Orr, Cara Lynn Hallermann, Wendy Funk, Val Therevas Ward and Carlos Escalante. Your smiles were a huge help.

My Facebook friends who came out in full force to send me so many positive messages throughout this journey that I'm surprised my heart hasn't burst yet. Also, my Facebook fusion and SI Joint support groups especially Julie Ewing, Jonny Wexler, Erica, and Denise. Thank you for taking a call from a stranger and guiding me.

The Hills Fitness staff for their ongoing support.

The yoga team at The World of Tennis in Lakeway, Texas: Melinda Kirchhoff, Anne Westcott Dandrid, Sarah

Breedlove, Lauren Creath, Sarah Walters and Kim Charlet. Thank you for teaching me it was okay just to show up.

The Mercy Health and Fitness in Clive, Iowa team and my new community of pool warriors: Pam Avaux, Judi Vogel, Jean Neibergall, and all the special people who helped me to keep showing up to the pool even when it was -30 outside. Your stories kept me showing up.

Sr. Jeremy Dempsey, O.S.B. and Sr. Mary Faith Schuster, O.S.B.—my writing professors in college and the seeds that started all of this. They saw hope where I didn't.

Oprah Winfrey, Sister Joan Chittister, Caitlin Clark and Brene Brown—some of my greatest inspirations, and whose books and talks and basketball games have kept me persevering through everything.

Acorn Publishing, and specifically Jessica Hammett who always believed my story mattered. I couldn't have finished this without your coaching.

The faces. There are so many people who I don't have names for, but whose faces I've memorized. Your nods of encouragement and comments that made me laugh or gave me peace are etched in my memory and keep me going on the hard days.

Finn, my guardian angel, my soul pup. Dang, I'm so grateful for you.

And Hope: I don't know your last name, but you were the first message of hope I received when I forgot hope was there.

About the Author

Pat Henneberry is an inspirational marketing executive, motivational speaker, and award-winning diamond industry expert with extensive experience telling captivating stories.

Throughout her career, Pat has worked with world-class brands including DeBeers and Tiffany, helping transform the diamond industry. She is the founder of The Jewelry Coach, a high-level consulting and training business, and she has written columns for *National Jeweler*'s "Coach's Corner."

Pat resides in Austin, Texas, with her sweet rescue pup Finn. She is an avid sailor, open-water swimmer, and a hold-my-drink-and-watch-me-do-this kind of gal. In her free time, she coaches a Special Olympics swim team.

Pat's Power Playlist

1. Brighter Days – Blessing Offor
2. Hold On To Me – Lauren Daigle
3. Landslide – Fleetwood Mac
4. Hold Me Closer – Elton John
5. Cold Heart (PNAU Remix) – Elton John
6. Love Me Anyway – P!nk
7. Hold My Hand – Lady Gaga
8. Fire and Rain – James Taylor
9. Rise Up – Andra Day
10. God Only Knows (Timbaland Remix) – for KING & COUNTRY
11. Lovely Day – Bill Withers
12. Rescue – Lauren Daigle
13. Bridge Over Troubled Water – Shaun Escoffery
14. Let it Be – JP Cooper
15. Remedy – Adele
16. O-o-h Child – The Five Stairsteps
17. Good as Hell (feat. Ariana Grande) [Remix] – Lizzo

www.ingramcontent.com/pod-product-compliance
Lightning Source LLC
Chambersburg PA
CBHW030404130626
46549CB00004B/1630